CONTENT

S0-BNT-795

ACKNOWLEDGMENTS

I would like to dedicate this book to three women who played a vital role in my life. The first is my mother, Stella Stanford, who while a single parent struggling against great odds, emphasized the need, and stimulated the desire for a proper education.

The second is my Aunt Nora Benjamin, who helped significantly toward achieving this end. Finally to Criselda Horne who as my health teacher greatly encouraged me to pursue Natural Health. She also helped open important doors and contacts for me in this field. I also express appreciation to Dara Dietz who has offered me valuable help with the art for the cover page.

May God richly bless them all, and help that through this book their influence, like a pebble thrown in a lake, may never end, but rather extend in ever-widening circles of blessing to the boundless shores of eternity.

FOR EDUCATIONAL PURPOSES ONLY

This book's objective is to furnish the reader with knowledge of the traditional use of natural medicinal remedies. It is not the intention of the author to diagnose and/or prescribe for sickness in any way, directly or indirectly, that is forbidden by the law. The intention is to share the gospel of health and of preventive medicine and to build or restore health, that your body may be healthy and be pain and disease-free—a true temple for Almighty God. Many health authorities and nutritionists hold very different and often conflicting views today. The author believes that Nature and God know best. Armed with the information in this book, you may cooperate with your doctor. If, however, you choose to exercise your constitutional right to diagnose, self-prescribe and / or treat independent of your doctor, then the author and publisher assume no responsibility beyond that of promoting the Gospel of health.

PART ONE

RADIO HEALTH GEMS
FROM DR. STANFORD

"When thou sittest to eat with a ruler, consider diligently what is before thee: And put a knife to thy throat, if thou be a man given to appetite. Be not desirous of his dainties: for they are deceitful meat." Prov. 23:1-3

FOOD FOR THOUGHT

Did you know that today in the typical diet of "sophisticated", "civilized" man, that there is often a cobra under the table — a deadly hidden killer?

HOW TO KILL YOUR LOVED ONES WITH FOOD

Did you know that you can kill your family and loved ones and actually receive sympathy from your friends and others instead of blame? Here is how to do it.

Use coffee on rising in the morning instead of peppermint tea or lemon juice water or orange juice. For breakfast let the toast be white bread — the whiter the more effective. Don't ever buy whole wheat or whole-grain bread—Who likes that coarse, dry bread anyway? To whip up the nervous system, sweeten the coffee with white sugar instead of honey. White sugar is a terrible health destroyer, but they will never suspect your motives. Put some more on the table for them to help themselves.

A good start. But the breakfast is not yet sufficiently lethal. You need cholesterol and saturated fat. Get two eggs for an omelet and something worse. Let us see, what shall that be? Oh yes I have the answer. Some ham or beef would do the job. The ham is preferable, because pork is the most toxic of the regular flesh meats consumed and thus more tasty. Spice it up well. Use plenty of harmful spices: black and white pepper, mustard, MSG, etc.

Throw in a dash of vinegar. Any vinegar (except apple cider vinegar) will destroy red blood cells and make them anemic, while the cholesterol will clog up their arteries to prepare them for a stroke or heart attack. With this idea in mind, fry the omelet with butter, instead of olive oil. Use enough to let the food swim in the oil or butter.

Now remember that this is the way to do it. Just make sure you give this to them daily, if you can get away with it, or at least as often as you can. They will think you the best chef in the world. Don't be stingy with the salt.

Now use the same principles for the other meals. Use lots of processed, refined commercial foods. Give them pizza and fast foods whenever you can get away with it, for they are even more deadly than the breakfast you prepared. Those restaurant cooks and famous chefs are secret killers too, so don't feel too guilty. They are even more deadly with their food preparations and this is why they are hired with a good salary to do their job. In fact, if you learn this lesson well you may qualify to become a world famous chef one day too — a professional, secret, unsuspected killer.

Now let's continue. The key is to be generous with animal proteins and grease and do plenty of frying. (If they complain of too much meat, tell them they need lots of proteins to be healthy, that vegetarians are sickly, that they need vitamin B12). Give them their meals at irregular times each day. That will harm them too, just like having many combinations at the same meal.

Maybe the husband is ungrateful and a complainer. Then the kids are so rebellious. Well take some revenge: Lots of soda and cola drinks loaded with white sugar. Fruits and vegetables must only rarely appear on the menu. And when you select them, make sure you do not get fresh, well-ripened ones. Why not? Come on now, don't get dumb on me! If the fruits are fresh and well ripened, they will be tasty and have a lot of nutrients. Don't forget your plan is to kill, not to lengthen life. Select fruits that are half dead and tasteless then they will hate fruits (a plus for you). Make sure you fuss with them to eat them.

Again, don't give them raw salads— that will strengthen them. If they ask for them, cook the vegetables until all the health-building enzymes are destroyed and the precious vitamins and minerals are gone. Boil the vegetables in plenty of water for a long time and make sure you throw away the water. Well, you may drink some of the water for all your hard work, but do it in secret. If they see you and do likewise they will receive valuable minerals and live longer, which is contrary to what you want. Right?

Let's move on. Ensure that ice-cream and rich deserts are liberally supplied, otherwise you are not doing a good job. This is serious business. Candies and chips and curls etc., must never be missing. To test your skills, urge them till they overeat. Give the kids money generously to buy these snacks.

If you are impatient for results, give them a good scolding at mealtimes as often as you can get away with it. It will upset their digestion and undermine their health. They probably deserve it anyway.

Now here is another secret for their faster demise. Let the evening meal be the heaviest instead of the lightest. Let them eat late, and go to bed late. How? Use your imagination. Let them watch television or something. Alcohol and wine must always be okay. Give your husband cigarettes to relax.

By now you should start expecting results. Buy a black dress for the funeral, or a bright red one if you prefer that color to celebrate your success. Tempt him to excesses at night — Never say "no." Anything to weaken him. He's probably cheating on you anyway. Put him to rest. The rebellious kids should follow shortly after.

Now don't be discouraged. Some may have a strong constitution and that will take a little longer to break down. Be persistent: "quitters never win, and winners never quit" says the proverb. As they begin to complain of aches and pains, don't hesitate to give them prescription or commercial drugs. Leave those natural herbs alone. If they ask for them, say that you have no confidence in those quacks who call themselves natural doctors. Who likes those bitter herbs and nasty-tasting roots anyway?

Again, don't quit. The wise ancients said, "Success is not a happening but a result . . . it is doing instead of doubting and working hard instead of wishing." Keep at your job: kill them with food, little by little while they keep praising you as a wonderful chef. You will not fail. Soon, yes soon, success will be yours. And do you know the best part? The police will never suspect a thing. See that you cry a lot at the funeral, and repeatedly ask God why He allowed this to happen to you, that it is not fair. Do a good job at it and none but you and the good Lord will ever know that you killed them -with **food.**

(HEALTH GEM #1)

THE TRUE CAUSES OF DISEASES

Did you know that although there are thousands of diseases today, that the basic underlying causes of them all are amazingly few? They involve the mental, emotional and physical stresses, abuses and excesses of an artificial lifestyle. More specifically, these factors are as follows:

1. Defective nutrition as in the indulgence of overstimulating and harmful foods such as refined fragmented foods like white sugar, white flour, white rice(foods that have been robbed of priceless nutrients and re placed with toxic substitutes and additives) animal proteins and saturated fats.
2. Poisons and pollutants in the air, water and especially the in the food that we take into our bodies.
3. Overstimulation or overindulgence in eating, pleasure-seeking, sex, work, etc., without taking adequate rest.
4. Lack of exercise and poor elimination of toxins from the system.

These factors in time provoke profound biochemical and metabolic derangement and weaken the immune system. It is in this condition that opportunistic disease germs overpower the body's weakened defenses and disease is established in the system.

Do not be deceived dear friends. The cause and prevalence of disease are not mystical and inexplicable, as some medics in their own financial interest try to make it appear. Bacteria and virus are not the primary cause of disease. They come in the picture as a result of our decadent, self-destructive habits of living and eating. The function of these bacteria is to help return to the earth and recycle organisms that are fast becoming or already have become disqualified to live.

Hence dear friends, eliminate these health destroying factors and habits from your life and with the cause removed, Nature will quickly restore the miracle of health. Not that we effected a cure. We just removed the cause — so logically, by taking away the reason for its existence, the problem of disease disappears and health is restored.

(HEALTH GEM #2)

A MISUNDERSTOOD FRIEND

Did you know that what we commonly call "disease" is really a friendly, self-defensive reaction by our bodies? It is a protective effort from the system; a protest against the abuses of nature's health laws, to which we have been subjecting our bodies.

Do you know that without pain to warn us that we would frightfully and irreparably injure and kill ourselves? Think of accidentally putting your hand on something very hot, or stepping on something very sharp and not feeling any pain? What would happen to the hand, if pain did not grab your attention and trigger a reflex to pull it away from the burning object? Thus, pain really is a friendly, defensive reaction.

In reality pain, fever, diarrhea, loss of appetite, fatigue and other similar symptoms that we label disease, are only efforts of nature to undo the terrible effects of stresses and toxins that we force upon it. It is an effort to restore more healthy conditions. The pain is designed to grab our attention and secure our cooperation as the body makes an effort to restore more healthy conditions.

But how do we in our ignorance generally react? We become alarmed and seek to suppress these manifestations. We hurry to get some drug to remove the cold. We seek to lower the fever and force food upon one with no appetite.

Poor humans! When shall we learn? Do you know that through colds, the body eliminates a lot of toxins, phlegm and mucus? Do you know that fever, unless it is extremely high, helps the body's defenses against infection, and that occasional fasting (or skipping a few meals) strengthens the system, as long as you take enough water or health juices? Have you noticed that when animals are sick (dogs, cats, lions, tigers) they instinctively refrain from eating for a while, and try to eat grass (herbs)? Shall we be less intelligent (dumb) than the dumb animals?

Yes poor humans, instead of helping nature, we suppress these symptoms, we stifle the body's defenses and as a result we lay the foundation for the more chronic degenerative conditions like arthritis, high blood pressure, tumors, arteriosclerosis etc.

Well in closing let me shock you somewhat by saying, in the language of doctor Paavo Airola, that we actually "need" disease to get well. By now, it should not be hard to figure that out.

So what have we learned? Do not stifle nature's self-defensive, health-restoring actions with drugs and ignorance. Instead, let's cooperate with nature (through cleansing diets of fresh fruits and vegetables and natural herbs and occasional fasting) and we will enjoy much better health.

(HEALTH GEM #3)

ARE DRUGS THE ANSWER?

Did you know that drugs never cure disease? No, they certainly do not. They often kill bacteria and virus, but they also poison, weaken and kill many healthy cells in the body. Removing or changing the symptoms of a disease, does not cure the disease while the cause remains. Do not be deceived friends. In reality, except for severe emergencies and trauma, they cause the body far more harm and stress than the conditions they are trying to correct.

Many thousands of people die every year in our hospitals from iatrogenic (caused by drugs and doctors) diseases. Let us take aspirin for instance. With its less familiar chemical name acetylsalicylic acid, we find that it is especially used by millions of arthritic and other sufferers. Aspirin's popularity is based upon the fact that it alleviates pain, thus helping its consumers to feel better; it is cheap, easily available without prescription, and is widely considered as non-addictive and even harmless.

Interestingly, though viewed as non-addictive, it has become a perennial remedy for arthritics, and used in progressively larger quantities until they are virtually dependent upon the drug. Indeed, millions pounds of aspirin are sold annually in the U.S. of which amount arthritics account for a large percentage. According to the Journal of the American Medical Association, even as far back as Nov. 15, 1947 it was known that aspirin, including many other patented drugs containing it, may cause severe poisoning and provoke pathological changes in the brain, liver and kidneys. With longstanding use, aspirin may depress the production rate of the immune bodies of the organism and thus debilitate the body's healing mechanism.

It has been found that even small doses of aspirin may cause cardiac weakness with an excessive pulse rate, edematous swelling of the mucous membranes, irregular pulse, and sometimes albuminuria (J.A.M.A. 1911). Besides its toxic effects, aspirin tends to promote bleeding and delirium, restlessness and/or confusion and according to research it is known as a vitamin destroyer. Aspirin has been found responsible for the destruction of large quantities of vitamin C in the body. Believe it friends, most other drugs are not better, but treacherously worse.

Then why are drugs so popular today in medicine? The answer is very simple indeed. Money — yes the drug industry is a billion-dollar business. And since money corrupts, should you be surprised that the disease-industry today is very corrupt? And do you think that a corrupt disease industry is more interested in your health than in their money —

their megabucks? I leave you to decide friends. But I advise you to watch out for your own health. Analyze the filtered information given on the regular media and go beneath the surface.

From years of experience internationally as a health practitioner, I know that the hardest and most frustrating cases for persons to regain health, are where they have used drug medication for a considerable period of time.

Be wise dear friends. Learn of alterative medicine. I would stay away from drugs like from a rattlesnake. Nutrition is the greatest single factor that determines health. I close this gem with the words of the great father of medicine, Hippocrates: "Let your food be your medicine, and your medicine be your food." Drugs are definitely not the answer to health.

"Wherefore do ye spend money for that which is not bread? And your labor for that which satisfieth not? Harken diligently unto me, and eat ye that which is good" . . . Isaiah 55:2. This is good and godly advice friends. Follow it.

(HEALTH GEM #4)

A KILLER FOOD (Part 1)

Did you know that one of the most popular foods today is a killer food? Yes and what would that food be? The answer is white sugar. Oh yes, it certainly is very destructive to health—a killer food. In fact in large quantities, it is even more harmful to health than animal proteins. It greatly clogs the system and debilitates the immune system.

But how can such a sweet and innocent substance be harmful? Here is a quotation from the Pan American Diet Book, by G.W. Remsburg:

"Granulated or white sugar is deficient in organic salts and nutrients because of the process of refining, and when taken into the body breaks down the cells in order to furnish the blood with the necessary alkaline elements to neutralize the carbonic acid which is formed by the oxidation of the carbon of which the sugar is composed. Sugar is almost pure carbon."

In reality sugar does much more harm than I have the time to tell here. It provokes over-acidity of the stomach. It depletes the system of minerals, upsetting the alkaline balance, clogging the system and rendering the blood toxic.

What then can you use for sweeteners? Use natural, unfragmented sweeteners: honey, dates, raisins etc. The natural sugars found in fruits and vegetables are single molecules that are easily digested and assimilated by the body. They are good for us. Common table sugar on the other hand(sucrose), has a double molecule which is very hard to breakdown. It severely irritates and thus weakens the intestinal tract. Raw cane sugar is less harmful than white sugar.

So what is the point to remember today? Use natural sweeteners like honey, dates, raisins or the like and stay away from white sugar which is as habit-forming and treacherous as any narcotic. It is a killer food.

- By the way, when used moderately, honey is an excellent food that has been used for thousands of years — actually since Bible times. Pay no attention to would-be-experts who try to tell you otherwise.

- Honey is a sedative, laxative, emollient, bactericide, preservative, good for kidneys, burns, bed-wetting, nerves, colds, asthma, sinusitis, prevents nutritional anemia, and increases calcium retention in the system. In mod eration it's good. Use it instead of killer sweets like sugar.

(HEALTH GEM #5)

A KILLER FOOD (Part 2)

Did you know that although white sugar is very dangerous to health, as explained in part one, that in the U.S. today it has reached the dangerous level of 126 pounds per person per year? Not only does it weaken the immune system and deplete the body of essential minerals and vitamins, but it does even more damage. Here is a quotation from Dr. Phillip M. Lovell, of the Los Angeles Times:

> "Commercial sugar is representative of the ultimate extreme in food degeneration. To just merely state that it is a starvation food is putting it very mildly. The term food is certainly a misnomer. Sugar is the most poisonous and injurious product in our nation's diet with no exceptions and under every possible condition."

> "These facts assume special importance when it is pointed out that more than 65 percent of the animals slaughtered for the markets are swine. Therefore, the slaughterhouse products being used in processing sugar are derivatives of pork."

This last point about pork products, alludes to the sugar manufacturing process in which blood albumin from the slaughter house is used to carry away any protein matter which clings to it. Bone-black or animal charcoal also is used [ironically] to help 'purify' the sugar. So now you know that even pork products from the slaughterhouse are used in the commercial preparation of sugar. And some of you think you are good vegetarians, don't you?

Dr. Sandi Mitchell (Ph.D.) in an article "Sugar, Our Nation's Unnatural Disaster," shares the following:

> "Sugar acts upon the tissues like a chemical substance, such as an acid or caustic. A bit of raw flesh placed in a strong solution of sugar soon becomes shrunken in appearance because of the abstraction of water which the sugar absorbs. Candy, ice cream, pastries, etc., because of the sugar irritate the mucous membrane of the stomach, and thus cause many degenerating problems."

Now in closing I repeat the following counsel. Use natural sweeteners like honey (especially raw honey) dates, raisins, prunes, etc. These promote good health. Do not use chemical sugar substitutes like saccharin, etc. They are even worse. And remember, commercial sugar is a killer food, shun it like the dangerous drug that technically it really is.

(HEALTH GEM #6)

A THIEF OF GOOD HEALTH

Did you know that there is a health problem even more common than the common cold, one that afflicts almost the entire human race? What is this problem? It is constipation. Constipation is where the bowels fail to move as often as the number of meals eaten daily— generally it is having less than two or three bowel movements daily, as all natural health experts will tell you.

Constipation is a serious matter: it is a thief of good health. The waste matter, which is thus left entirely to long in the body, imparts a toxic quality to the blood which circulates these waste poisons all over the body—affecting every organ and every cell. Someone has truly said that chronic constipation (which causes toxemia) is the mother of nearly every disease: - arthritis, tumors, and cancers are just a few on the interminable list.

What are some common symptoms of constipation? Offensive breath, coated tongue, backache, headache, mental dullness, insomnia, depression, loss of appetite and frequent pains here and there. When the bowels of infants move irregularly, they are often irritable.

To avoid constipation we need to know and avoid the causes. The principal cause is a wrong diet: a diet of refined, processed, fragmented foods with not enough of the fiber that is so plentifully found in fruits and vegetables. Other causes include: lack of sufficient exercise, not drinking enough water (dehydration) hypothyroidism, sluggish liver, overeating which provokes fermentation, gas and constipation, frequent neglect of the calls of nature; overuse of laxatives, constant worry, anxiety, grief and nervousness, also too much animal protein which provokes putrefaction and then constipation and toxemia.

Still others consist of partaking of too many varieties at one meal, not masticating food sufficiently, overcooking foods, using foods that are too concentrated, as well as the use of constipating liquids like coffee, tea and alcohol. Drinking with meals, and/or eating too much soft, mushy foods, are serious contributory factors also. The causes must be removed before chronic constipation can ever be overcome. Especially so are a wrong diet and lack of exercise.

Foods that combat constipation include: figs, dates, prunes, raisins—more fruits and vegetables in general— especially high-fiber foods. Raw foods, whole grains, raw seeds and nuts, and especially sprouted seeds are very highly recommended.

Do not use commercial laxatives. They do harm. Herbal laxatives include the following: cascara sagrada or sacred bark, senna pod or leaf, alder, buckthorn bark, dandelion, mandrake, slippery elm bark, flax seed, psyllium seed or husks, ginger, raspberry leaf etc. Any good herbal book like "Back to Eden" by Jethro Kloss will give the dosages.

A daily bath as well as a cup of warm herb tea or lemon juice water without sugar upon arising in the morning, helps combat constipation. Keep your bowels open and clean for vibrant health.

(HEALTH GEM #7)

FOOD FOR THOUGHT

Did you know that of all the countless creatures that inhabit planet earth, that man is the only one who destroys his food with heat and chemicals before he eats it? And that consequently, man is the only one who needs so many hospitals?

RAW VERSUS COOKED

Did you know that raw foods are much superior to, and actually digest faster than cooked foods? Did you know that man is the only creature in Nature that destroys his food before he eats it? Consequently, only man needs so many hospitals and health clinics.

While cooking renders food more palatable to our generally perverted appetite, it destroys vitamins, enzymes and minerals and creates more acid wastes in the system. Most foods are cooked only because of tradition. Grains are benefitted by being cooked, even though many grains can be soaked overnight and be used uncooked with soybean milk, or almond butter or homemade spread. This may sound revolutionary, but it is a healthy reality.

Here are some statistics for example, shared by Dr. Paavo Airola, researched in the world-famous Max Plank Institute in Germany:

"Vegetable proteins are higher in biological value than animal proteins. For example proteins in potatoes are biologically superior to proteins in meat, eggs or milk."

"Raw proteins have higher biological value than cooked proteins. You need only one-half the amount of proteins if you eat raw vegetable proteins instead of cooked animal proteins."

Between 70 and 80% of your diet should consist of natural, uncooked foods. If you suffer from any serious disease, use 90 to 100% uncooked foods for a few months, for faster and more certain recovery. Start with small amounts if you are not accustomed, then gradually but persistently increase the amount to the desired level.

Raw foods are highly cleansing and therapeutic. They preserve the biochemical structure of amino acids (proteins) and fatty acids which facilitate digestion. Cooking, on the other hand, changes these foods chemically, complicates their digestion and produces more waste.

Sprouting beans, grains and seeds is an excellent way to use raw grains and with very great benefit for the system. People who live in tropical countries can at certain times in the year, eat almost 100% uncooked foods with great benefit to health. This may not be feasible for those who live in colder climates, unless you are very knowledgeable in natural health nutrition.

So what is our point to remember today? Eat lots of raw foods; chew them thoroughly and enjoy a tremendous boost in health. In general, "if something can be eaten raw, rarely should it be cooked."

(HEALTH GEM #8)

FOOD FOR THOUGHT
"Raw proteins have higher biological value than cooked proteins. You need only one-half the amount of proteins if you eat raw vegetable proteins instead of cooked animal proteins." Dr. P. Airola.

MY CRUEL STEPMOTHER

People say that she is my mother but no, no, that could never be. She could not be my true mother. I stoutly maintain that to this day, she must be my stepmother. No true mother would treat her own child so meanly. She must have adopted me some unfortunate day. I prefer to call her my stepmother—my cruel stepmother.

Now let me explain and when I am finished you will be able to recognize my awful stepmother though she often hides herself under different faces. Actually my name is Estómago (Spanish name for stomach), not an exciting name I admit, but I work very hard for my inconsiderate guardian. Without me her life would be impossible, but does she care about that?

In the morning on getting up, instead of giving me some nice warm lemonade with one or half a lemon and a bit of honey if she cares, which will cleanse, refresh me and give me a good start, she gives me a dirty, but popular drink called coffee. O I really can't tell you how awfully unhealthful that stuff really is! What it does to me and to my brother and friends, is even worse. It excites our poor nerves then correspondingly depresses them after the effects of the drug caffeine are worn off. Any wonder that my stepmother is a nervous wreck?

It weakens me even before my day's job properly begins, and it irritates and stresses brother Heart. While the dinghy-looking coffee drink makes her feel better, it really makes me miserable. And because I don't like to complain so early in the morning she thinks that everything is all right. Oh sometimes how I wished good old common sense was sold in the supermarkets.

Now what is her idea of a decent breakfast? Do I get some nice whole grain homemade cereal, healthy toast with fruits or vegetables and preferably non-dairy cream? Oh no! You would think that with a master's degree she would be more enlightened, but no, indeed. Why would she be so kind to me, anyway, she didn't make me? So I get some smelly, scrambled eggs, liberally spiced with salt, black pepper, vinegar and mustard, all swimming around in butter and oil. This with white bread, mayonnaise and ham. Oh my stepmother is mean! My most mortal enemies are present in the breakfast.

My stepmother's second meal begins around nine o'clock and ends at about five o' clock in the afternoon, just in time to prepare for supper. (By the way they call her Mildred). Boy, is she cruel! Every few minutes she is eating something. Never did a slave work harder than she makes me work. She is so cruel you would think she was a gangster, but oh no she goes to church, and very regularly too. She calls herself a deaconess. I secretly doubt that: a deaconess would be more temperate and self-controlled. In the church there used to be an old minister that preached   that gluttons would go to hell, and that your body was the temple of God. Not too many people liked him. At least Mildred didn't. She much prefers the new minister who teaches that the "kingdom of God is not meat and drink (though he looks like six months pregnant) but love in the Spirit."

Like I said, every few minutes, Mildred is eating. They talk about child abuse in this country, I think there should be a law against stomach abuse. The only problem is that then nearly the whole American population would have to be arrested. My average capacity is about one and a half pint. I work best when I have a little free space, since my muscles must constantly churn and massage the food to mix it well with my digestive enzymes. But cruel Mildred eats and eats and eats until I feel like a stuffed bear. I often feel paralyzed. The result? Fermentation, irritation, gas, indigestion, constipation, and sour stomach. Mildred has a relative named sister Tell-The-Truth. She told Mildred that she had a strong breath problem. Wow, does Mildred like her! Yet instead of treating me better, she keeps blaming all the new germs, viruses and pollutants in the air, especially in these big cities.

With all the bad food combination, the injurious spices, the refined sugars, the vinegar, mustard, preservatives, you would think my stepmother would understand why I would get sick. Common sense would tell her to skip a meal or two for a few days or, better still, to go on a fruit diet for a week or two to give my overworked tissues an opportunity to repair their damages and remove the debilitating toxins. When I am suffering from her gluttony, instead of giving me some charcoal (A best friend when one has stomach poisons with fermentation and gas), or some good stomach herb like wormwood, angelica, caraway, goldenseal, comfrey, anise or even peppermint and/or ginger tea, all my good pals, she gives me some awful and dangerous chemical mixtures that destroy my health. She calls them antacids. I think they should be called devil-acids for I am sure the devil invented them.

Believe it friends, Mildred is not only cruel but sometimes she is dumb, dumb, dumb. Let me explain. You already know Mildred has a halitosis problem, only it is getting worse. Not surprisingly she is always constipated. She gets a bowel movement every two or three days. The reason is her diet that is too refined and processed, and too rich in animal proteins fat and grease. Then she washes down the food with soda, coca cola and such like. So I get sick and there is a lot of fermentation and gas. After seven to ten hours instead of three to five, with a normal healthy meal, with nice raw salads, I pass the food onto Sister intestines and Brother Colon. Poor Brother Colon, he is a mess! — yes it is with him that the putrefaction really gets down to business.

Mildred's colon is awful. Talk about putrefaction and gas. Is she a candidate for colon cancer? When Mildred fires gas, everybody disappears for full 15 minutes. In fact, I believe even the skunk would run if it happened to be there. Her bad diet has killed out nearly all the friendly acidophilus bacteria, which help in the digestion of food and the production of vitamins like B12. Consequently, there are mostly only the unfriendly, putrefactive bacteria in her colon, billions of them. And actually the more they flourish, the more they overpower the friendly bacteria. What a vicious cycle indeed!

Poor Brother Colon, I feel so sorry for him: at times he smells likes a cesspool. When Mildred speaks to people, they often take a step backward. But do you think she gets the message and talks less? Do you think she treats brother Colon or myself any better? Think again! Poor dumb Mildred, instead of giving brother Colon a good two weeks of wormwood, cascara sagrada, flaxseed, senna or some good herbal colon formula, she is forever wasting her money on breath-freshener and Lysol deodorant. The worse part is that she says that she has a master's degree. I can't help thinking at times like her Guyanese cousin would say, "Well look what a Master's degree has come to!"

But actually I don't believe it. Someone that qualified would know that the foul, putrefying gases from the colon diffuse into the blood and are taken around the body. In the lungs some of it passes and escapes when she speaks. She still doesn't understand the causes of her halitosis. She is still hung up on the Luis Pasteur germ-is-the-cause-of-all-health-problems notion. So my stepmother blames the germs in the air for this problem. If only I had the courage I would tell her to throw away her master's degree and take some common sense lessons from the lower animals — the cow, for instance.

Now please don't think I am mean. No, I really am not. I do have much respect for the cow. I really do. In fact, sometimes I think I would be better off being a cow's stomach for the cow chews its cud thoroughly, but my stepmother! She is too mean to do that, she must make my worker harder, she swallows big, large pieces and so quickly that I cry for mercy. Does she hear or care? Often I am amazed that she doesn't choke more often, she seems to just inhale the food.

I often wonder, why did my stepmother choose me for adoption?

Why me? Why did not some sensible, balanced, Godfearing man or woman? But I really don't want to fly in the face of the Almighty. I must accept my lot. But oh yes, I wish sometimes that Mildred would read good books on health and nutrition and learn to care for her body. Poor Milly, she doesn't know how to cook properly so as not to destroy the nutrients in the food, but she is taking French and Music classes. O that she would read a good health book like for instance, "The Entering Wedge: The Genesis of Diet and Health."p. 41, 42 which would explain her sour breath problem. Let me just quote two paragraphs to support my point:

"Suppose you leave a little food in your breakfast dish, then at lunch add more to it, but again not use up the whole, and repeat this again and again, day after day. Can you imagine how the plate and the food will look and smell in a few days? Yet a person who eats between meals, eats before the previously taken food leaves the stomach, is unconsciously creating a condition that is just as bad."

"If given no chance to empty from one meal to the next, the stomach is bound to ferment and produce gas and toxins, so that what little energy is realized from the food, the system must use to throw out the poisons. Rather than take food between meals, flush your stomach with pure fresh water — promote a good healthy appetite for the next meal. Moreover, if after a reasonable length of time all the food has not left your stomach, rather than eat only because the regular time for meal has come or only because you have a false hunger, keep on drinking warm water until your stomach becomes light and your appetite stimulated. Correct eating habits make one's earnings go further, promoting health, increase energy, sweeten the breath, and develop amiability. What gain without having to invest!"

But alas my stepmother does not like books like these. She finds them boring and says they make her feel guilty. She prefers the classics and to read about the political situation in the Middle East. That is outside of her T.V. hours, of course,

In truth, entire books can be written about Mildred, my friends. There is no doubt about that — true and interesting biographies. And they would easily be bestsellers too. Let me just share one bit of information about Mildred, that would be a highlight in her biography, for instance. Call it a testimony if you like. You will like it and learn a lesson from it anyway. I learned too. I learned one valuable lesson: I learned that I should never laugh at Mildred! Boy, is she vindictive!

Let me explain. You see Mildred has a weight problem— Not surprising when you consider the way she eats. Now having met this potentially new boy friend, she decided to lose some weight. It so happened that Mildred had an old scale that she did not realize was defective. The reading it gave was about 8-10 pounds less than correct. Mildred loved that scale. One day, however, just about the time she met Mr. New boyfriend, it gave up the ghost, stopping altogether. So Mildred had to buy a new scale. Mildred believed the new scale was defective and exchanged it for a better one. When again, with some trepidation, she climbed on the newer scale, she flew into such a rage that she threw it right through the window unto the pavement. It broke like a thunderbolt into countless pieces. Boy, did I laugh! I thought that I would die with laughter, it was so funny, I cracked up, I really did.

Alas, Alas! I think my stepmother must have heard me laughing and decided to take some revenge on me. She invited Pastor Love-a-Dinner over and fixed a large pot of Italian pasta and she really gave it to me. How I groaned and moaned. She paid me no mind. But the worse was still to come. I tell you friends, Mildred is cruel.

Do you know what she did when her guest left? The eating party (a nightmare for me) started all over again. The half pot of pasta that was left for the next day, she put it on the table and really shoved it into me. I did not know that such torture could even exist. Oh I was in agony for days. I wouldn't dare laugh at Mildred again. O no I really wouldn't. My stepmother is really a stomach abuser. She is cruel. But by the way, do you know her? Does she wear your face sometimes? Why do I have this funny feeling that she is very familiar to you? Hi Mildred!

(HEALTH LECTURE)

TIPS FOR A STRONG AND HEALTHY STOMACH

1. Start the day with some warm herbal tea or lemonade without sugar: a little honey may be used.
2. Eat at regular hours. Three meals a day for normal persons, for many persons two are even better.
3. Space meals five to six hours apart. Never eat between meals. If before the work is done, more food is pushed upon it, fermentation, gas, poor digestion and sour stomach often result.
4. Drink water ideally 60 to 45 minutes before or 1 ½ to 2 hours after meals. Drinking with meals dilutes the digestive enzymes and creates havoc with the job. This is also one reason for poor digestion, fermentation and intestinal problems.
5. Don't combine raw fruits and raw vegetables in the same meal: They need different enzyme combinations. Otherwise digestion is impaired and a lot of toxins are generated. Avoid more than two or three dishes in the same meal. Often there is war in the stomach from many combinations. Then one suffers awfully and produces gas and toxins.
6. Raw foods, properly chewed, do wonderfully for the stomach's health. They are rich in enzymes and are cleansing and therapeutic. They increase the micro-electric tension in the cells and thus invigorate, rejuvenate them, in this way increasing their life span.
7. A stomach's bitterest enemies are the following: white sugar (which pass along undigested to the small intestines after considerably irritating the delicate lining), grease, (raw olive oil on foods is okay), black pepper, rich cakes, pastry, and highly seasoned food, animal products, mustard, vinegar (it destroys red blood corpuscles) and other hot spicy condiments. They greatly inflame and weaken the delicate membranes.
8. Garlic, onions, caraway, anise, thyme, ginger, capsicum, (cayenne) help digestion. Raw salads make digestion easier. Lemon juice and garlic in combination, assist digestion wonderfully. Use them liberally, alone or combined.
9. Leave the dangerous commercial antacids alone. They are loaded with harmful aluminum. For indigestion let her use 1-3 tablespoons of charcoal (when it is activated it is even better), or use any of the good stomach herbs mentioned earlier.
10. Finally. Never eat if very anxious, hurried, scared or tired or stressed out. The food only ferments. The stomach works very closely with the brain and endocrine system. For a clear brain it must be treated well.

When the stomach is miserable, it affects the whole body and your mood is likewise affected. Eat heavier meals earlier in the day. The evening meals should be light. Heavy evening meals often cause nightmares and are dangerous to health. Eat in a relaxed friendly atmosphere and digestion is better. Treat your stomach well and it will be your willing, faithful servant forever.

BEVERAGES

Did you know that the best beverage is pure, clean water? Water is the beverage that the all-wise creator provided for all the creatures of nature. Spring water is still the best. Failure to drink between 6-8 glasses of water every day, is the primary cause of constipation, kidney problems and poor health in many persons.

Lack of enough water causes the blood to be in a poor and toxic condition. The urine becomes too concentrated and the kidneys suffer. In fact, the elimination of waste products from the system is greatly impeded and every organ in the body suffers when enough water is not taken into the system. Gall stones and kidney stones also form more readily in the body.

Why should not water or other beverages be taken with meals? Because it dilutes the digestive juices and thus provokes fermentation, acid stomach, poor digestion and resulting constipation. Cold liquids taken with meals do even more harm, since the stomach works best at a certain temperature which cold liquids disturb. Drink water or juices without added sugar, between meals. Do not wash down your foods with liquids if you want good health. This habit is difficult to break, because everywhere people drink with their meals and everywhere people are sick for violating the laws of health. Chew your food thoroughly, very thoroughly and mix it with saliva which is highly alkaline and thus promotes good digestion.

People who eat largely of animal products, people who use much salt, drug medications, pepper, spices and condiments, require considerably more water to cleanse the system of the unhealthy substances. Harmful beverages include coffee, tea, cola drinks, soda and every drink made with white sugar or its chemical substitutes. White sugar is the most health-destructive food article in use today. Coffee seriously weakens the nervous system and will make you an addict and a nervous wreck in time. In place of coffee use herbal teas sweetened with some honey. For example, use: peppermint, spearmint, chamomile, lemon grass, ginger, red clover, etc. Use natural fruit or vegetable juices, without adding cane sugar. And by the way, seawater is beneficial to health when used both internally and eternally.

What is the point to remember? Water and other liquids should be taken between meals. Take them about 45 to 60 minutes before, or 90 to 120 minutes after eating, depending on the general effectiveness of your digestion. This means you should wait a longer time if your digestion is usually slow. Chew your food thoroughly; Mix it well with saliva and use healthy, herbal tonic teas like peppermint and/or red clover teas, instead of coffee which is so dangerous to health.

Again, stay away from white sugar drinks like from poisons. Use 6-8 glasses of water daily. Avoid prolonged drinking of distilled or rain water (which is dead, having no minerals). The reason is that, contrary to some "experts" the body can absorb with benefit some minerals found in natural waters. Positively, natural spring waters are best.

(HEALTH GEM #9)

FOOD FOR THOUGHT

By taking a glass or two of warm water on getting up in the morning, you can prepare the stomach and its digestive juices for efficient digestion. Add the juice of a lemon for better results. Drinking a glass or two of water about 35—40 minutes before mealtime can help control an unruly appetite?

WATER— THE QUEEN OF BEVERAGES

Did you know that ...
• At most you can live only 10—12 days without water even in a cool place?

• Whether you are in the Arctic or in a desert, in order for your lungs to utilize air, it must be warm and moist? Drinking enough water ensures this.

• An adequate water intake prevents your skin from becoming too dry?

• Water is absolutely essential to flush out toxins from the system? Drinking enough water helps protect against the hazards of the changing seasons and weather.

• Water cushions the bones at the joints, thus facilitating bodily locomotion?

• Water is a natural diuretic, very essential for overworked or eased kidneys?

• Adequate water intake helps prevent kidney infection, by preventing over concentrated urine?

• Used internally and /or externally, water can help control a fever and its complications?

• An adequate water intake (along with clean diapers), helps prevent severe diaper rash?

• By taking a glass or two of warm water on getting up in the morning, you can prepare the stomach and its digestive juices for efficient digesttion. Add the juice of a lemon for better results. Drinking a glass or two of water about 35 — 40 minutes before mealtime can help control an unruly appetite?

(HEALTH GEM #10)

HYDROTHERAPY - THE MIRACLE OF WATER

Did you know that one of the most powerful agents for combating sickness and restoring health is the skillful use of hot or cold water? — hydrotherapy. In fact, there is no other agent, no drug, that is as versatile or as effective for things like water.

1. Water is a sedative. Unlike sedative drugs, it can lessen the action of the heart and soothe the nervous system, with no negative side effects. There is no drug, further, that will decrease the temperature of the body as quickly and as efficiently as water. With a cool or cold bath the pulse can be reduced from 40 - 20 beats in a few minutes. Heat can also be similarly reduced.
2. Water is an anodyne. It will lessen pain and nervous sensibilities. A hot water fomentation never fails to alleviate pain. A warm bath soothes the nerves and combats insomnia.
3. As an astringent, cold water is often used to stop bleeding.
4. Water is a good laxative - drink 6- 8 glasses of water daily between meals to combat constipation.
5. Water is an antispasmodic. In hysterical convulsions, cramps and in fantile or puerperal convulsions, water is very effective.
6. As a diaphoretic, warm or hot water can produce copious perspiration.
7. As an eliminator - water is the greatest solvent known. It is perfect for dissolving toxic waste matter and debris in the body preparatory to elimination.
8. As an alterative which strengthens and promotes health, not mercury, or any other drug for that matter, could rival water.
9. As a stimulant, tonic and derivative, the use of hot or cold water is marvelously efficacious. Is it not amazing how the best things in life cost little or nothing? Is it not wonderful how the beneficent Creator freely placed the great healing agents of water, air and sunshine at the disposition of all his creatures?

I trust dear friends that you will seek to become intelligent as to the effective use of water to build health — hydrotherapy. If you are interested in taking a correspondence course on this and like subjects, contact: Sunny Mtn. School of Natural Medicine, P.O. Box 119, Mountaindale, NY 12763. And REMEMBER drink 6-8 glasses of water daily to prosper and be in good health.

(HEALTH GEM #11)

GETTING SICK TO GET WELL

Did you know that in natural medicine that a healing crisis frequently occurs before complete health restoration takes place? What is this and why? This healing crisis refers to the condition in which the patient temporarily feels worse before a complete cure is effected.

"But how can this be?", a person usually asks. Now that I am eating better and following these cleansing programs, how is it that I am feeling worse? The explanation is actually very simple. Because juice-fasting and cleansing herbal programs are so effective, they dissolve tremendous quantities of toxins that have been accumulated and hidden away in the system. These dissolved toxins are thrown into the bloodstream in the natural course of things in preparation for elimination from the body.

With such large quantities of waste matter and toxins in the bloodstream the organs responsible for elimination — the kidneys, liver, lungs and skin - become overloaded and this is what causes the temporary manifestations that are called the healing crisis. The person may experience headaches, skin eruptions, catarrh, fever, etc. Properly understood, however, there is no cause for alarm. It is really a good sign. It means that the body is actually responding effectively to the cleansing programs. These discomforts will be temporary and notable improvements will soon be observed. One way to control the rate of cleansing and the intensity of the cleansing reaction, is by repeated, short intermittent juice-fasting instead of a long, uninterrupted one.

It must be stressed again and again, that all true healing comes from within the body itself - Nature's own internal forces. The role of the true doctor is to create an internal environment or suitable condition to facilitate this. Drugs do not provide this congenial environment. They generally poison the system and change the manifestation of the disease from one form to one that is worse. While they may destroy germs, they also poison body cells. Drugs never cure — be not deceived. In cases where healing takes place, it does so in spite of the drug, rather than because of it. Natural or biological medicine, is what is in harmony with nature.

People must become intelligent to these things and not be deceived by conventional mass media propaganda. Nature is the true healer — cooperate with Nature and enjoy vibrant health. And finally, remember that with natural remedies a healing crisis is a good sign. The temporary discomfort is a sign of imminent better health.

(HEALTH GEM #12)

EXPOSING THE LIE

Two health experts lived in town. One an M.D. from a famous school of medicine, the other an ordinary citizen - an expert in natural health and nutrition. Now Mrs. Very-Sick paid them a visit. The diagnosis? A malignant tumor in the right kidney. Dr. Famous-Surgeon explained that she could easily live on one kidney and that the only way to save her life was an operation to take out the diseased kidney. Mr. Natural-Health expert on the other hand was fortunately able to persuade this daughter of common sense to adopt a different approach: to try his natural health program. Result? In three months, Mrs. Very-Sick was a brand new woman with two healthy, happy, tumor-free kidneys.

Now please tell us Judge Common-Sense, which of these two men is the TRUE doctor? Who better deserves the name? One who is a brilliant expert in cutting out our organs, but does not know how to help us keep them healthy, or one who knows how to teach us to keep our organs intact and healthy and to restore their health if lost. Well you heard him answer.

"But what if Mr. Natural-Health expert only studied two years, what if he never went to a famous, 'accredited school?' "

"All the more credit to him," says Judge Common-sense. "If he is an expert in the field of restoring health, then he is the true doctor."

"Since this scenario is repeated almost daily in our world today, who would you say is the real 'quack' here judge Good-Sense if I may change your name?"

"Well, with all due respect to Dr. Brilliant-Surgeon, I beg to defer answering this question."

Did you know that we have all, for too long, been brainwashed into believing that to effectively cure the sick (to be a doctor) you need many long and tiring years of study: umpteen years studying bacteria and viruses, slugs and snails, and drugs, drugs, drugs? And oh yes lots of voluminous books featuring the names of countless diseases with their almost unpronounceable Latin names. We have been made to believe that only these superbrilliant men, after wearisome years of study at the greatest universities can successfully understand disease and cure the sick. This is the BIG lie, the myth to be exploded.

It is indeed about time that the adulterous relationship between Orthodox Medicine and the Drug-Industry come to an end; it is about time they stop peddling their false, moneymaking propaganda throughout the western academic world.

Do you know that if you are diligent in your studies and you understand the principles of any good Natural Medicine program that in two years or less you (an average person with average common sense) will have learnt enough to be able to restore health in more than 90% of the world's diseases? Actually, this is NO exaggeration. The cornerstone of health is nutrition and not drugs? Do you know that conventional medical doctors generally do not study nutrition? Shocking, isn't it?

Did you know that over the past two centuries that drug medications and unnecessary surgeries have sent as many people to an untimely grave as compared to both world wars combined? Is it not time we come to our senses to stop idolizing and paying blind homage to a moneymaking system that depreciates and debilitates the human race? Shall we not learn to be original, independent thinkers, with inquiring minds or shall we be content to be educated weaklings merely reflecting and practicing conventional or traditional wisdom as long as we can get some money and prestige out of it? Shall we let our minds be so weak, so washed, so cowardly that we dare not deviate from the beaten path of modern medical conventionality and its academic fallacies?

Fortunately, if you are doing any such eye-opening health course. It is your privilege to cultivate breath of mind and depth of convictions. You can dare to be different; dare to be the proud progeny of common sense, as revealed in the above story.

Can it be good sense, dear student, that you should spend 5-8 years studying squids and mollusca, bacteria and viruses, political science and art, and drugs and more drugs (along with all the other irrelevant subjects in the modern curriculum for medical doctors) and after that still not know how to keep people healthy with their organs intact, but be brilliant experts in cutting out those organs? Is it not infinitely better to study the vital principles of Preventive Medicine and Natural Health that can effectively solve the vast majority of the world's health problems?

We assure you, that these points are no exaggeration. More of these points will be understood in [2]the course. All experienced natural health doctors will confirm what is said here and in time you will discover it. I have personally successful restored health, through natural remedies, to persons who were scheduled to have their organs removed and know exactly what I am saying.

Should we not seek to love and elevate the human race, rather than depreciate and debilitate it. We love our M.D. partners. They are certainly not bad people. They are just an inseparable part of a corrupt, moneymaking system with a tunnel vision on drugs. They look to drugs and surgery for the answer to virtually every health problem. In all fairness, though, they are good for emergencies and accidents. Other health problems? Oh NO: they would drug and/or cut you to death. They are

Footnote 2 alludes to Natural Doctor's Health course done at Sunny Mtn. School of Natural Medicine.

also generally very intolerant of alternative medicine. As a potential doctor you must not allow yourself to be brainwashed. No, not for money, prestige or fame. Be a friend and healer of the race by becoming a true Natural Health Doctor. Why not follow the footsteps of the great divine Healer who once walked the dusty streets of Palestine healing "all manner of diseases."

(HEALTH GEM #13)

UNTOLD GRATITUDE

Modern medicine expresses untold gratitude for the enormous business increases generated by you our popular patrons. We are so glad that you accept our modern miracle drugs. How worried we were that you would not subject yourselves to their many toxic side effects! In fact, we often hide this information from you for this reason. We are happily amazed that you couldn't care less, such is your confidence in our system.

The Natural Health Experts say that what you eat has everything to do with your health. Never mind those nuts. Our position as conventional medical doctors is the opposite: "Eat whatever you want—it has nothing to do with your health." We are happy that you are sensible enough to believe us. (Have we not spent billions of dollars and umpteen years researching these matter?) What loyal patrons you are. No, no, don't listen to those quacks. Enjoy your fried chicken, steak, eggs, and all your animal products, etc. Don't forget your ice-cream and the processed and refined foods, which since they are "enriched" are a boon to your health.

You assure us that we will never be out of business. Come with your heart problems, your cancers and tumors. We will slash, burn and drug them out as our opponents often describe our therapy. We prefer the more scientific, polite and nice-sounding, medical terms "surgery," "radiation" and "chemotherapy." If you have to sell your houses to pay the bill before dying anyway, are you not happy that we did our best? And what if you lose a few years of life, because your system could not respond to our program! If you are New age, you would reincarnate (as a pretty bird or even a frog), won't you? Or if a Christian, wouldn't you go straight to heaven? You are so smart and understanding, how can we thank you enough! We will only bill you for 'curing your loved ones until they die.'"

Indeed, we close with sincere words of "untold gratitude" for your undying faithfulness and loyalty to us and our wonderful, modern miracle drugs. Keep it up "till death do us part."

(HEALTH GEM #14)

ISN'T MILK VERY GOOD FOR YOU?

There are health authorities today who insist that milk is a wonderful and indispensable food for human health, while other equally convincing experts contend that milk is very poorly digested in humans and that it results in fermentation with lots of impurities in the system, and that milk is also mucous producing food.

It is further, argued that milk is not good for human consumption, because it is not "natural"—that is, the milk was designed by nature for baby animals; that after weaning, no other creatures of nature use milk. Non-milk advocates stress that milk, especially raw milk, is hazardous to health since it constitutes an ideal medium for pathogenic microbes. Finally, milk is condemned by many because today's milk is loaded with antibiotics, hormones, pesticide residues, drugs and chemicals. Well, what is the truth?

In his book "Are You Confused?", Dr. Airola, truly a reputable nutritionist of enormous research, elucidates these moot questions very convincingly. He explains that ironically, both sides are right to some extent, but that their claims are also exaggerated. Objectively speaking, for countless centuries man has used milk in the diet with significant health benefits, but the truth is that not all can digest milk well.

Research has shown that those races that had milk as a part of their diet for unnumbered generations, tend to utilize and digest milk quite well. On the other hand, where milk was not a historic part of the diet, those peoples are generally more deficient in the enzymes for adequate milk digestion.

People of European descent or from the Middle East, also the East African Nilotic Negroes are genetically programmed to use and digest milk effectively. On the other hand, peoples like the Eskimos, Australian Aborigines, American Indians, people from China, New Guinea, and the Phillippines are not genetically programmed to digest milk properly. Certain enzymes like lactase, are lacking. More specifically, while more than 95% of white Americans digest and use milk without problems, 75% of Black Americans have demonstrated milk intolerance.

While raw milk is indeed an excellent medium for the proliferation of pathogenic bacteria, pasteurization as mentioned before, destroys vital elements in milk and changes the chemical properties of certain nutrients, rendering them more difficult to digest and assimilate. Health experts also warn, and appropriately so, that much of the milk processed in the industrialized nations today, is loaded with residues of detergents, pesticides, herbicides, toxic and dangerous chemicals and drugs, and is thus unsuitable for, and potentially hazardous to human health. These researchers believe only the highest quality, uncontaminated, raw milk from healthy animals should be used.

Milk in its soured form like yogurt, kefir, acidophilus milk etc., is superior to sweet milk. Being predigested it is very readily assimilated and has a very positive and health-promoting influence on the intestinal tract. More specifically, it enhances the growth of friendly acidophilus bacteria (intestinal flora), thus inhibiting putrefaction and constipation. Further, goat's milk is considered much superior to cow's milk. Not only is it non mucous-forming, its protein and mineral ratio are more close to human milk. It has more thiamine and niacin, with proteins of a higher biological quality than those of cow's milk. The fat in goat's milk, besides, is naturally homogenized, which facilitates digestion.

Protein in milk, is biologically superior to all other forms of animal proteins. It has been found to be more "complete," and its casein is a most excellent quality protein. Not only is its protein more easily digested and more effectively utilized in the system than proteins in eggs or meat, but also the milk, in contrast to meat, does not burden the system with such toxic wastes like purine and uric acid.

Finally, as additional empirical testimony in favor of the great health benefits of clean, uncontaminated, raw milk, many of the peoples already cited as famous for good health like the Russians, Bulgarians, Scandinavians etc., have for centuries been liberal in their consumption of milk. It is also noteworthy that virtually all European medical researchers, scientists and nutritionists who have studied the milk issue in detail, recommend milk as an important component of the dietary regimen.

(HEALTH GEM #15)

FOOD COMBINATIONS

Today, in the science of healthful nutrition, there are still more and more discoveries being made. Current research is uncovering other dynamic principles of nutrition that significantly impact health. One such principle has to do with food-combinations. It has been found that different foods (like each fruit and vegetable) need different enzyme combinations for their digestion, and that mixing many foods indiscriminately, often results in poor digestion, fermentation and constipation. That is, mixing fewer foods at the same meal, promotes more effective digestion and assimilation.

For example, it is well known that proper protein digestion requires an abundance of hydrochloric acid in the stomach to begin breaking down the peptide bonds and to deactivate the salivary amylase. In a carbohydrate-rich meal there is a less copious secretion of hydrochloric acid. Researchers in this area explain that when the stomach is largely filled with a carbohydrate meal like a large raw salad, for instance, and then you eat a protein dish at the end like a slice of ham, that protein dish (ham) will most likely be poorly or partially digested, because enough hydrochloric acid was not secreted by the stomach.

Consistent with this principle, it is recommended that it is better to eat protein foods first on an empty stomach, thus stimulating a copious secretion of hydrochloric acid, then add carbohydrate foods. That is, eat your ham or steak or protein-rich food first, and then the salad. Or at least, the advice is, let the protein food (whether tortilla and beans or steak) be eaten with the salads. After you try it, no doubt, you will discover that it not only makes sense logically, but it actually works, and you have fewer stomach problems.

Research in the area of food combinations is still relatively young, and there are, consequently, still areas of controversy. However, almost all authorities in this area agree that generally raw fruits and vegetables should not be combined in the same meal. (There are a few exceptions to the rule of course). As mentioned before, these foods involve very diverse enzyme combinations for effective digestion and therefore such indiscriminate combinations are not recommended at the same meal. They result in gas and ineffective digestion. It is recommended to eat at least one fruit meal and one vegetable meal daily. Some special or exceptional fruits that can be used with almost anything include: lemons, avocado, papaya and pineapple. Grains, nuts and seeds may be well combined with fruits or vegetables.

Persons who do a great deal of intellectual work and persons of sedentary habits are especially benefited by following these healthful rec-ommendations, as their digestive systems are generally more sensitive. Regular exercise in the open air tends to promote digestion, especially when some attention is given to proper food combination.

(HEALTH GEM #16)

PART TWO

GLOSSARY OF MEDICINAL PROPERTIES OF HERBS

ABORTIFACIENT
An agent that induces or causes premature expulsion of a fetus. Examples: pennyroyal, cotton bark and seeds.

ALTERATIVE
An agent which produces gradual beneficial change in the body, usually by improving nutrition, without having any marked specific effect and without causing evacuation. Examples: sumac (bark or leaves), red clover, golden seal, ginseng.

ANALGESIC
A substance which relieves or minimizes pain an anodyne.
Examples: wintergreen, meadowsweet, willow.

ANAPHRODISIAC
An agent which reduces sexual desire or potency. Examples: black willow, skullcap, cucumber, hops, belladonna.

ANODYNE
An agent that soothes or relieves pain. Examples: comfrey, chamomile, hops, mullein, catnip, sassafras.

ANTHELMINTIC
An agent that destroys or expels intestinal worms; vermicide; vermifuge. Examples: garlic, pomegranate, hyssop, papaya or pumpkin seeds, woodsage.

ANTIBILIOUS
An agent that combats biliousness. Biliousness here referring to a class of symptoms comprising nausea, abdominal discomfort, constipation, headache, and gas caused by excessive secretion of bile. Examples: dandelion, mandrake.

ANTIBIOTIC
An agent that inhibits the growth of germs, bacteria and other harmful microbes. Examples: garlic, Iceland moss, sundew.

ANTIEMETIC
An agent that counteracts nausea and relieves vomiting. Examples: Anise, barley, ginger, clove, peppermint, golden seal, hops.

ANTILITHIC
An agent which reduces or suppresses urinary calculi (stones), and acts to dissolve those already present. Examples: kidney beans, golden rod, birch, cucumber, buchu leaves, holly, pimpernel.

ANTIPERIODIC
An agent which combats or protects against periodic or intermittent diseases like malaria. Examples: Golden seal, blue vervain, quinine, boneset, angelica.

ANTIPHLOGISTIC
An agent which reduces inflammation. Examples: Witch hazel, cucumber, fenugreek, golden seal.

ANTIPYRETIC
An agent which prevents or reduces fever; febrifuge, refrigerant. Examples: hops, garlic, fenugreek, lemons, sumac.

ANTISCORBUTIC
A source of vitamin C for curing or preventing scurvy. Examples: Sarsaparilla, lemons, citrus fruits.

ANTISEPTIC
An agent for destroying or inhibiting pathogenic or putrefactive bacteria. Examples: garlic, eucalyptus, myrrh, wintergreen, golden seal, thyme.

ANTISPASMODIC
An agent that relieves or checks spasms or cramps. Examples: black cohosh, rue, mullein, garlic, camomile, eucalyptus.

ANTISYPHILITIC
An agent that combats syphilis. Examples: sarsaparilla, poke root.

ANTITUSSIVE
An agent that relieves coughing. Examples: licorice, onion, slippery elm, okra, flax seed, parsley, plantain, lemons.

APERIENT
A mild stimulant for the bowels; a gentle purgative. Examples: dandelion, golden seal, rhubarb.

APHRODISIAC
An agent for arousing or increasing sexual desire or potency. Examples: artichoke, celery, cloves, coriander.

AROMATIC
A substance having an agreeable odor and stimulating qualities. Examples: dill, cinnamon, catnip, wormwood, nutmeg.

ASTRINGENT
An agent that contract organic tissue, reducing secretions or discharges. Examples: lemon juice, nettle red pepper (cayenne), sumac.

BALSAM
A soothing or healing agent; A resinous substance obtained from the exudations of various trees and used in medicinal preparations. Examples: spikenard, balm of Gilead.

CARDIAC
An agent that stimulates or otherwise affects the heart. Examples: black cohosh, raspberry, wormwood, valerian, hawthorn.

CARMINATIVE
An agent for expelling gas from the intestines. Examples: dill, angelica, garlic, pumpkin seeds, catnip, hyssop, peppermint, spearmint, valerian, calamus root.

CATHARTIC
An agent that acts to empty the bowels; when mild—laxative. Examples: mandrake, castor bean. Laxative: figs, golden seal, senna (leaves), cayenne.

CEPHALIC
Referring to diseases affecting the head and the upper part of the body. Examples: sumac berries, rosemary.

CHOLAGOGUE
An agent for increasing the flow of bile into the intestines. Examples: radish, mandrake, centaury, garlic.

CONDIMENT
A herb that enhances the flavor of food. Examples: peppers, ginger, dill, garlic, onions.

DEMULCENT
A herb that soothes irritated tissue, particularly the mucous membranes. They make excellent poultices. Examples: figs, comfrey, mullein, ginseng, okra, flaxseed.

DEOBSTRUENT
An agent that removes obstructions, by opening the natural passages or pores of the body. Examples: golden seal, nutmeg.

DEPURATIVE
An agent that cleanses and purifies the system, especially the blood. Examples: dandelion, red clover, Echinacea, lemons.

DETERGENT
An agent that cleanses wounds and sores of dead or diseased matter. Examples: red clover, golden seal, psyllium.

DIAPHORETIC
An agent that promotes perspiration; sudorific. Examples: ginger, elecampane, dill, sassafras.

DIURETIC
An agent that increases the secretion and expulsion of urine. Examples: dandelion, celery, golden rod, nettle, juniper, sassafras, strawberry.

EMOLLIENT
An agent used externally to soften and soothe. Examples: adder's tongue, almonds, aloes, Althea (marshmallow), figs, mullein, flaxseed, fenugreek.

EMETIC
An agent that causes vomiting. Examples: mustard, milkweed, alder(black, red, smooth), bloodroot, blue vervain, boneset.

EMMENAGOGUE
An agent that promotes menstrual flow. Examples: camomile, rue, thyme, mint.

EXANTHEMATOUS
Relating to skin diseases or eruptions. Examples: dandelion, red clover.

EXPECTORANT
An agent that promotes the discharge of mucous from the respiratory passages. Examples: garlic, hyssop, vervain, eucalyptus, balm of Gilead.

HEMOSTATIC
An agent that stops bleeding. Examples: plantain, comfrey, alder, lemons, ergot, knotweed, nettle, tormentil, witch hazel.

HEPATIC
A agent that acts on the liver. Examples: dandelion, bittersweet.

HYPNOTIC
An agent that promotes or induces sleep. Examples: hops, camomile, valerian, catnip, lady's slipper, skullcap.

MATURATING
An agent that promotes the maturing or bringing to a head of boils, carbuncles, etc. Examples: flaxseed, burdock leaves.

MUCILAGINOUS
An agent that produces a gummy or gelatinous substance in medicinal preparations. Examples: flaxseed, fenugreek.

NARCOTIC
A substance which relieves pain and induces sleep when used in medicinal doses; in large doses narcotics produce convulsions, coma, or death. Examples: mistletoe, belladonna, celandine, henbane.

NERVINE
An agent that has a soothing or calming effect on the nerves; formerly an agent that acts on the nervous system. Examples: peppermint, hops, camomile, skullcap, mistletoe, celery, red clover, cinchona bark, valerian, peach leaves, skunk cabbage, lady's slipper.

OPTHALMICUM
A remedy for the diseases of the eyes. Examples: golden seal, dandelion, eyebright.

PARTURIENT
A substance that induces and produces labor. Examples: Red pepper, red raspberry.

PECTORAL
A remedy for pulmonary or other chest diseases. Examples: nettle, mullein, flaxseed; slippery elm.

PURGATIVE
An agent that produces a vigorous emptying of the bowels. Examples: rhubarb, psyllium, milkweed, celandine.

RESOLVENT
Promotes the resolving or removing of abnormal growths, such as a tumor. Examples: thyme, pokeroot, mandrake.

RUBEFACIENT
A gentle local irritant that produces reddening of the skin. Examples: bloodroot, buttercup, cowslip, juniper, horseradish.
SIALOGUE
Promotes the flow of saliva. Examples: ginger, nutmeg.

SUDORIFIC, SOPORIFIC
See Diaphoretic.

STIMULANT
An agent that excites or quickens the activity of physiological processes. Examples: sassafras, cayenne, eucalyptus, ginger, wintergreen, celery.

STOMACHIC
An agent that strengthens, stimulates, or tones the stomach. Examples: papaya, slippery elm, cayenne, dandelion, camomile, ginseng.

STYPTIC
An agent that contracts tissues; astringent; specifically, a hemostatic agent that stops bleeding by contracting the blood vessels. Examples: witch hazel, shepherd's purse.

TONIC
An agent that strengthens or invigorates organs of the entire organism. Examples: golden seal, dandelion, vervain, thyme.

VASOCONSTRICTOR
An agent that narrows the blood vessels, thus raising the blood pressure. Examples: Anise, hawthorn, rosemary, motherworth.

VASODILATOR
An agent that widens the blood vessels, thus lowering blood pressure. Examples: garlic, boneset, onion, parsley, skullcap, blue cohosh.

VERMICIDE
An agent that destroys intestinal worms. See anthelmintic.

VERMIFUGE
An agent that causes the expulsion of intestinal worms. Examples: bird's tongue, American centaury, blue vervain.

VULNERARY
A agent that promotes the healing of wounds. Examples: aloes, plantains, vervain, papaya, myrrh, mullein.

GATHERING AND PRESERVING HERBS

The first system of healing that the world has ever known, even from bible times, was herbal. In the Bible herbs are mentioned quite often. Man was placed in a garden and given "every herb yielding seed" for his "meat." Genesis 1:29. In the book of Revelation is described the "tree of life yielding her fruit every month, whose leaves are for the healing of the nations." Revelation 22:2.

Again, in Genesis 3:28, man was instructed to eat the "herb of the field," after he was driven out the garden. In Ezekiel 47:12, there is another reference to the healing benefit of the leaves. Several places speak of the balm of Gilead, while in the New Testament, in Luke 11:42, mint and rue are mentioned as familiar herbs.

Herbal medicine continued to be very widely used for millennia until around the 16 th century, when Theophrastus Von Hohenheim began using chemicals which gradually increased in popularity. People began relying upon the fast-acting chemical poisons and less upon the slower, but safer and more reliable herbs. It is said that the Saxon invaders brought a great deal of knowledge of herbal medicine when they invaded Great Britain. Also many native peoples of the world like the American Indians, though without knowledge of biology or chemistry, were amazingly conversant with different herbs that effectively cured diseases, which today still defy and humble modern allopathic medicine.

There are great healing benefits from herbs. Indeed, as said before, herbs are really a class of foods, and therefore are an extension of nutrition. Herbs should, however, be gathered carefully, since a few herbs are poisonous. In fact, the FDA Consumer, October 1983, cautioned: "If you gather your own herbs to brew a cup of tea, be absolutely, 100 percent certain that the herb you pick is the herb you seek . . . There are half a million known plant species. Less than 1 percent are poisonous. But it takes only one error." This is good advice.

So clearly the gathering of herbs requires experience. The preservation and preparation of herbs are likewise of much importance, for by careless inattention, or ignorance, great harm or even fatal consequences may result. By careful methods the herbs retain their medicinal properties and yield marvelous results.

The richness and quality of herbs, like fruits and vegetables vary with the richness and quality of the soil in which they are grown. Those growing in the wild tend to be more potent than those that are cultivated. Herbs are best gathered in the dry season, when the seeds are getting ripe or the plant is in full bloom. Various parts of the same plant may have different chemical or medicinal properties. All parts of plants, however, are used in herbal medicine: roots, barks, flowers, seeds, fruits and leaves.

Roots should be dug when they possess their sap, in spring when it is rising or in the fall, when it has descended. They should be cut into pieces and dried in the shade. Barks should be gathered in the spring when the sap is rising. The rough outer portion should be removed and the inner bark retrieved. You may put it in the sun for a short time. All parts of herbs must be thoroughly dried for adequate preservation, but overexposure to sunlight will reduce their nutritive or medicinal properties. Leaves, flowers and seeds should be gathered when they are at their best. Do not gather defective ones. When thoroughly dried, heavy brown paper bags are best for their preservation. Some herbs if properly dried and stored, can retain their medicinal properties for years. Nonetheless, the fresher herbs are generally better.

PREPARATION AND USE OF HERBS

Herbs are commonly used in the form of teas, salves, ointments, liniments, tinctures, syrups and poultices. Herbal preparations should be fresh for each day apart from the ointments, liniments, salves and tinctures. Though herbs may not be as fast-acting as drugs, it cannot be overemphasized that the careless or excessive use of some herbs can be toxic or hazardous to health. Thus, proper instructions regarding dosages must be respected.

Tea preparations are of two kinds. Infusion and decoction. An infusion is made like regular tea. That is, in an infusion, the herbs are not boiled. Rather boiling water is poured upon the herbs, covered, then five to 20 minutes later, strained and used cool, warm, or hot as indicated or desired. If allowed to boil, and if not covered, some of the valuable properties may be lost or destroyed.

Steeping allows the aromatic and volatile ingredients and other nutrients to pass into the water from the herbs. Stems, twigs, and larger parts of plants should be cut into small pieces and steeped a little longer. The general dosage, unless otherwise indicated, is one teaspoon to a cup of water (or half to one ounce) to a pint of water. Glass, enamel or porcelain utensils are best for these purposes. One teaspoon of dried herbs corresponds to about three of fresh herbs. One to three cups, unless otherwise indicated, of the brew may be taken.

A decoction is usually made from the tougher parts of the plants—

roots and barks. It is made by simmering the part of the plant in water, preferably in a nonmetallic pot, from between 5 and 30 minutes. Roots should be simmered for half an hour or more, but never boil hard any decoction. One teaspoon of powdered herb or one tablespoon of cut herbs to a pint of water is the usual dosage.

For the amount of time you plan to simmer the herbs, you need to add that percentage of extra water to compensate for evaporation. This means if you will simmer a herb for 25 minutes, use an extra 25% more water for the amount to be lost in evaporation. The dosages are approximately the same as for infusion, unless otherwise indicated. Use your discretion: if you find them too strong in taste you can always add some water.

Tinctures are another popular way of using herbs. They are very concentrated extracts of herbs in liquid. They are made from potent herbs that are not ideal as teas—herbs that may have a disagreeable taste and may need to be used for a lengthy period. Tinctures are rubbed on the skin like ointments.

An extract is a highly concentrated liquid form of a herb that is usually 10 times more potent than a tincture. Extracts are made by cold percolation, by high pressure, or evaporation by heat. Different methods are used to correspond to the nature of the herbs. Extracts constitute convenient and commonly-used methods of storing and utilizing herbs. They act much more quickly than powdered herbs, teas or capsules. Six to eight drops (this equals one teaspoon of tincture), is the usual dosage.

Powdered herbs may be used with cold or hot water. Hot water effects a faster reaction. ½ a teaspoonful of the herb to ¼ glass of water is the regular dosage. A glass of warm or cold water may be drunk after the dose. Herbs may also be used in capsule forms.

It must be borne in mind that these dosages are for adults. The amount should be modified to, ½ or ¼ for children depending on their age, size and condition. Persons with sensitive stomachs or very weak persons may react strongly, or with excessive sensitivity to herbs. The problem is not the herbs, but the weakened, oversensitive condition of the person. In such cases the dose should be significantly reduced and gradually increased as tolerance builds up. Often the same dose may be given in smaller amounts over a period of a few hours during the course of the day.

Syrups are another popular form in which herbs are used. To make a herbal syrup, dissolve three pounds of brown sugar in a pint of water and boil until thick, you can then put in any medicinal herb. Bee's honey, or malt honey may be used in place of sugar. It must be boiled thick. Otherwise, it will sour. Salves are another effective way to use herbs. One half pound of finely cut herbs to 1 ½ pound of cocoa fat, or pure vegetable oil, with 4 ounces of beeswax may be used. Mix thoroughly and place in the sun or even on low heat for three to four hours. Strain and then use warm or cold.

Finally, herbs are used as liniments and especially as poultices. Poultices are excellent for any kind of inflamed glands, whether the groin, prostate, breast or neck. They are ideal for carbuncles, eruptions, abscesses and boils. A great many herbs are used for poultices, so they should be studied carefully. Flaxseed, hyssop, balm, cayenne pepper, flaxseed meal, red sage, comfrey, wintergreen, lobelia, chickweed, burdock, smartweed, charcoal and many other herbs make effective poultices.

Herbal liniments are excellent for all pains, painful swellings, skin eruption, pimples, bruises, boils, etc. They can be applied from every few minutes to every two hours.

Applied to the temples, the back of the neck and forehead, they can alleviate headaches. They are excellent for rheumatism, athletes' foot and toothache. For toothaches the liniment must be applied on the outside of the jaw, all around the gums and in the cavity. The mouth may also be rinsed with it. Herbal liniments may be used to relieve pain in any part of the body. An ounce of golden seal, 2 ounces of myrrh and once of cayenne pepper with 70 percent rubbing alcohol, make an excellent liniment. The method is simple. Mix together well the ingredients and let stand for one week, shaking every day then finally pouring off and bottling.

SEVEN FRUITS WITH POWERFUL MEDICINAL PROPERTIES

Since herbs are really another dimension of nutrition, and since herbology and nutrition work as perfect partners, the final aspect of this section will feature seven common fruits and seven common vegetables that are both popular foods and important herbs. They have a dual membership as it were. They are valuable foods in balanced nutrition, as well as very respected members of the herbology modality. These seven fruits discussed here are apples, bananas, figs, grapes, lemons, papaya and pomegranate. Our seven selected vegetables are cabbage, celery, cucumbers, dandelion greens, garlic, parsley, and pumpkins.

APPLES

Perhaps everyone today has heard of the saying: "An apple a day keeps the doctor away." The statement is actually a reflection on the wonderful nutrients and properties of the apple as a fruit, and the medicinal properties of both the fruit and parts of the tree like the bark. In fact, hieroglyphic writings found in the pyramids and tombs of ancient Egypt reveal that the apple was both a food and a medicine.

Apples contain generous amounts of calcium and have 50 percent more vitamin A, than oranges. They are very rich in vitamin G and have other vitamins. Apples have significant therapeutic properties. They are alkaline foods that facilitate elimination. The pectin content in apples, helps them absorb water in the bowels, providing desirable bulk and stimulating peristaltic movement and proper bowel movement. Apples are often used for low blood pressure and hardening of the arteries because they are considered good blood purifiers and are helpful to the lymphatic system.

The peelings from apples make a good tea. In fact, the peeled and grated apples are also effectively utilized in diarrhea. When the skins are consumed with the entire fruit, they are mildly laxative. Finally, while the fruit is diuretic and laxative, the bark is tonic and is a febrifuge.

BANANAS

Bananas were historically cultivated in India about four millennia ago. It is claimed that Spanish priests brought them to tropical America. The banana is a wonderful, popular and delicious fruit. In many South American countries, it is often cooked when green. When fully ripe, the banana has no trace of green, but is flecked with brown on the skin. The sugars in bananas are very easily assimilated when ripe. The fruit contains many minerals and vitamins. In one pound of bananas can be found, for instance, 1,300 IU of vitamin A, 24 mg calcium, 85 mg phosphorus, 1.8 mg iron; 1.7 mg niacin, 29 mg vitamin C, and small quantities of other nutrients.

Therapeutically, bananas are used for intestinal and gastric disturbances, since it is so very alkaline. They promote good intestinal flora (acidophilus bacteria) and supply much potassium. Bananas are sometimes used in reducing and detoxifying diets and even as poultice in the treatment of bee stings.

FIGS

Figs are native to western Asia and the Mediterranean areas—later spreading to the Middle East. Figs were popular fruits in Ancient civilizations, and are really wonderful and nutritious. The Romans took them to Europe and later the Spanish missions introduced them to California.

Figs are extremely alkaline. One pound of figs supplies 245 mg of calcium and 145 mg of phosphorus. Their high sugar content gives a boost of energy. Figs supply other nutrients as well. Medicinally they are described as laxative, demulcent, emollient and nutritive. It is the mucin and pectin that they possess, why they are laxative.

In the Bible the use of figs for poultice, is recorded when God himself through the prophet Isaiah directed that a lump of figs be placed upon king Hezekiah's wound and he was healed. Isaiah 38:21. Splitting open the fresh ripe fruit and laying it on a boil or a carbuncle, brings great relief. A tea made with the leaves is also used for a mouthwash, gargle, and skin problems. A syrup made of figs with or without a little lemon, makes an excellent cough medicine.

GRAPES

Like figs, grapes are one of the oldest fruits known to civilization and are mentioned repeatedly in the Bible. Grape seeds have even been found in mommy cases in Egyptian tombs dating back to more than three millennia. In fact, grapes and wine date back to prehistoric times. Amazingly between 6,000 and 8,000 varieties of grapes have been known, but only a small percentage are of commercial interest.

Four classes of grapes are recognized: table grapes, wine grapes, raisin grapes, and sweet, unfermented juice grapes. New York, California, Michigan and Washington are the principal grape-producing States. The therapeutic properties of grapes are widely known. In France, people often use grapes for entire days during the season with very cleansing results. The low incidence of cancer among these people, is linked with the medicinal properties of grapes. Grapes are high in magnesium which has a positive effect upon the bowels. Grapes are often recommended in reducing diets.

Grape skins and seeds are good for bulk, but can be irritating in conditions of colitis and ulcers. Hence persons with weak digestion or with ulcers or similar conditions should not consume these. Dark grapes are richer in iron. Grapes are very alkalinizing to the blood, and their generous water content is good for the system. They also have a soothing influence upon the nervous system. Crushed grapes have often been used as a pack on growth or tumors.

LEMONS

Lemons are indeed universally-prized fruits. They are native to Asia and have been cultivated there for more than 25 centuries. Lemons provide liberal quantities of calcium and vitamin C, also phosphorus. They are rich in potassium and vitamin B. Lemons and limes contain 5 and 6 % citric acid while oranges and grapefruits have 80% less.

Therapeutically, lemons constitute one of the most powerful alkalinizing foods. They are excellent to counteract many toxins in the system. They are especially good to detoxify the liver. When lemons are used, however, the eliminative organs should be working well to throw off the poisons that are stirred up. In throat and catarrhal conditions, lemons are excellent. Lemons are an excellent febrifuge, since a feverish body response better to citrus fruits than to any others.

Actually, a whole book can be written about the many virtues of lemons. Many natural health practitioners will tell you that lemons can be used with benefit in more than 100 diseases. There are very few diseases, indeed, where lemons cannot be used with benefit for their alkalinizing, detoxifying and other properties. Lemons' medicinal properties can be summed up as: antiseptic, antiscorbutic, antirheumatic, astringent, nutrient, febrifuge and stomachic. As astringents, lemons have also been used to arrest bleeding, especially of the nose.

PAPAYA

The papaya is originally from South America and later introduced to other parts of the world. It is an extremely nutritious fruit, very rich in vitamins A, C and E. It liberally supplies the minerals: calcium, phosphorus and some iron. In one pound of papaya can be found 5,320 IU of vitamin A, 170 mg of ascorbic acid, 49 mg of phosphorus, in addition to other nutrients and vitamins.

Therapeutically, the papaya is a stomachic, vermifuge, nutrient and vulnerary. It is especially known for its ability to facilitate digestion due to the presence of the enzyme papain which is similar to pepsin. Papaya is good for dyspepsia, and other digestive problems, since this enzyme is so effective. The milky juice from the unripe fruit can also be used to remove freckles, and is a powerful vermifuge. By its ability to break down proteins, papaya often helps remove allergies.

POMEGRANATES

Another fruit well known to the ancients, is the pomegranate. The Bible and Sanskrit writings make frequent allusions to it. The word is a derivative of a Latin word meaning "apple with many seeds." The tree reaches a height of 12 to 20 feet and the fruit is about the size of an orange.

The juice of the pomegranate is best for bladder disorders and it has a slight purgative quality. Its medicinal properties are astringent and anthelmintic. The seeds have long been used for expelling tapeworms. As the rind is high in tannin, its makes an excellent astringent for internal use. Topically, it can be used for skin problems, diarrhea and as a vaginal douche. Large doses of the rind can cause cramps, vomiting and other disagreeable side effects.

FOOD FOR THOUGHT

Lemons constitute one of the most powerful cleansing foods. They are excellent to counteract many toxins in the system. They are especially good to detoxify the liver. When lemons are used, however, the eliminative organs should be working well to throw off the poisons that are stirred up. Start with small amounts if you are very toxic.

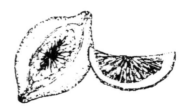

SEVEN MIRACLE VEGETABLES
WITH MEDICINAL QUALITIES

CABBAGE

This biennial herb of the mustard family, is native to Europe. It was cultivated by the ancients for more than four millennia. Over the centuries, other hybrids of the cabbage family have been developed: broccoli, Brussels sprouts, cauliflower, kale and kohlrabi. There are several varieties of cabbage: green, red, and white, with smooth or wrinkled leaves; and with round, flattened conical or oblong heads. California, Colorado, Florida, New York, Pennsylvania, Texas and Wisconsin are the largest cabbage-growing states.

Cabbage is a nutritious vegetable. It is rich in vitamin C and a fair source of vitamin A. It is high in calcium and thus is alkaline in its reaction in the body. It supplies many other minerals as well: potassium, phosphorus, sodium, chlorine, iodine and sulfur. Red cabbage has more calcium but a little less of the other minerals. The outer leaves of the cabbage may contain as much as 40% more calcium than the inner leaves.

Medicinally, cabbage can be effectively used as a pack for eczema, varicose veins and leg ulcers. Cabbage is laxative, and saukeraut or saukeraut juice, is excellent for sluggish intestines. The sulfur in cabbage helps destroy the ferments in the blood. Thus, cabbage is frequently used to relieve skin problems. Since sulfur tends to increase body heat, people with cold feet often receive benefit from its use. Cabbage juice is excellent for stomach ulcers. Again, empirical experience over the centuries has shown that cabbage helps to keep a clean, clear, healthy complexion.

CELERY

The celery is another vegetable that was widely used and prized by the ancients. It is native to the marshy regions ranging from Sweden southward to Algeria, Egypt and Ethiopia. Celery is high in water content and fiber and low in calories. It is a protective and an alkaline food. It supplies vitamin A, as well as vitamins B and G. It is rich in chlorine, potassium, magnesium and sodium.

Celery is a diuretic, stimulant and aromatic. It is excellent for acidosis, incontinence, liver troubles and dropsy. It is a fine tonic and encourages perspiration. In neuralgia, nervousness and rheumatism, it is indicated. As a flavoring agent celery is also much relished.

CUCUMBERS

Cucumbers have been cultivated and highly prized by ancient civilizations. There are references to them in the Bible. They are considered native to India. Cucumbers were popular with the Egyptians, Greeks and Romans. They are alkaline and non-starchy. Botanically, the cucumber (cucurbits) is more a fruit than a vegetable.

Medicinally, cucumbers are aperient and diuretic. Their ability to eliminate water from the body renders them excellent for persons with heart and kidney problems. The salad helps with chronic constipation, while the juice has a beneficial influence upon the intestines, lungs, kidneys and skin. For centuries, cucumbers have been used on the skin for cleansing and cosmetic purposes. It can also be applied to bed sores, and burns.

DANDELIONS

Dandelions are considered native to Asia and Europe and grow abundantly as weeds in the Eastern United States. The dandelion is a member of the sunflower family and there are hundreds of varieties. In the spring they furnish pollen and nectar for bees. They are very healthful greens. Dandelions are among the richest sources of vitamin A in the plant kingdom. In one pound of dandelions, there are 61,970 IU of vitamin A. Similarly, in one pound of the greens, there are 849 mg of calcium, 318 mg of phosphorus, 14.2 mg of iron and 163 mg of ascorbic acid in addition to smaller quantities of other minerals and vitamins. Dandelions are high in potassium, which makes the wild varieties bitter to the taste.

Dandelions have considerable medicinal properties. They are aperient, cholagogue, diuretic, stomachic and tonic. Dandelions enhance the formation of bile and remove excess water from the body in edemous conditions that develop from liver problems. The root of the dandelion promotes glandular secretions and by neutralizing and removing toxins form the system, it functions as a stimulant and tonic. Infusions of the root are said to be good for jaundice, gailstones and other liver conditions. Lukewarm dandelion tea has been recommended for constipation, fever, dyspepsia and hypochondria. Dandelions also relieve eczema and many skin conditions like rashes.

GARLIC

Garlic, like cucumbers, is mentioned in the Bible for being used by the early Egyptians for cooking and embalming purposes. It is actually native to Western Asia and the Mediterranean regions. Garlic, though associated with onion, is actually a member of the lily family. Its botanical name being Allium Sativum. This bulbous-rooted, perennial plant has been cultivated for centuries. The commonly-used bulb has a strong odor and acrid flavor, and is much more potent than the onion in its effects.

The medicinal praises of garlic have been sung from prehistoric times. Nearly all the great physicians of old have recommended it. Garlic is rich in sulfur. Medicinally, garlic's properties are very impressive indeed. It is anthelmintic, antibiotic, antiseptic, antispasmodic, carminative, cholagogue, digestive, diuretic, expectorant and febrifuge.

Like lemons, with which it is frequently combined therapeutically, garlic has a positively healthful influence in nearly every illness. It is used effectively to lower blood pressure, to expel worms and to treat goiter. In Europe it has been effectively used in the treatment of tuberculosis.

Garlic is an internal antiseptic. Its crotonaldehyde content is an effective bacteria-killer. Garlic regularizes the action of the liver and the gall bladder. Its tincture lowers blood pressure and combats arteriosclerosis. It has a positive influence upon the circulation and on the sexual organs.   The only problem with garlic, is the strong smell that you inherit along with its great benefits. The strong smell is reduced by eating it with greens like parsley. All things considered, however, garlic with its miraculous qualities, is one of nature's greatest gifts to man.

PARSLEY

Parsley was well known to the ancients. Its native country is considered to be southern Europe. This biennial plant is of two types. The foliage type which is more common and the turnip-rooted type. Parsley is available all year around to garnish or flavor dishes. Parsley is excellent in vegetable juices. It is high in iron and contains manganese and copper. It has an alkaline ash. Parsley possesses definite medicinal properties. It is an antispasmodic, carminative, diuretic, emmenagogue and expectorant. Parsley tea made from the seeds and the leaves, and also the fresh juice is indicated for cough, asthma, jaundice, dropsy, and painful or suppressed menstruation.

A tea made from crushed seeds will kill scalp parasites. Care should be exercised not to exceed the proper dosage, and parsley should not be used at all if the kidneys are in inflamed. Too much can irritate the kidneys. For gallstones, an infusion of the herb is effective. It is said to have a healthy influence upon the blood, brain and sexual system.

PUMPKIN

The pumpkin, like squashes, is native to North and South America. There is evidence that the early indigenous peoples living in North America cultivated the pumpkin. The pumpkin is really a squash botanically. They are very high in potassium and sodium and supply fair quantities of vitamins B and C. They are good in soft diets. Pumpkins are rich in vitamin A.

Medicinally, pumpkins are good to combat acidosis. They digest easily and are used in ulcers as a soft food. Pumpkins also have anthelmintic properties. The seeds of pumpkins, with some onion, mixed together with soy milk make a good remedy for worms in the intestinal tract. Soak three tablespoons of pumpkin seeds for three hours, then blend with half a small onion, a teaspoon honey, and half cup soy milk. This dose can be used three times daily. Pumpkins can also be used therapeutically as a poultice.

Considering that herbs supply nutrients like common foods, it follows that they are in fact, a class of foods and are thus included in Hippocrates' admonition: "Let your food be your medicine and your medicine be your food." I must emphasize, however, that there are poisonous plants and herbs and many herbs do have potent properties that in the hands of the careless or uninformed could produce sickness or even death. Nevertheless, all things considered, the skillful, informed use of herbs, like from the remotest times of antiquity, is a powerful therapeutic modality (and intimate friend of nutrition), that can effectively remove toxins and awake or stimulate the body's healing energies. Not surprisingly, all the pharmacopeias of the world today, include herbs, their extracts or by-products.

FOOD FOR THOUGHT

"If the doctors of today will not become the nutritionists of tomorrow, the nutritionists of today will become the doctors of tomorrow". Dr. Paavo Airola.

THE PROTEIN DEBATE

Now we are ready to look more closely at the protein debate. The questions naturally are, should one have a high-protein or low-protein diet; should it be animal protein or vegetable protein, and what proportions? Over the years this has been an area of tremendous controversy and confusion. No one questions the vital importance of this nutrient, but the opinions of the "experts" regarding its minimum daily requirement vary from 25 to 250 grams per day. The poor layman is left to take his pick based upon his sentiments, his taste or appetite for meat, or just his plain ignorance.

Again some insist that animal proteins are indispensable for vibrant health, and that on a complete vegetarian diet you will be malnourished and get sick, while others contend that a liberal flesh diet, is precisely the express ticket to ill health and degenerative disease. What is the truth on the subject? It is certainly interesting to trace the origin of the high-protein doctrine. The truth that our bodies are composed substantially of proteins, has added much credence to the, "you need lots of protein" conviction. However, much of the teaching and support for this position centers in the outdated 19-century research of certain German researchers whose works are still used freely in many universities today in the medical and nutrition departments.

The scientists: Von Liebig, Von Voit and Max Rubner, arrived at the incorrect conclusion that the Minimum Daily Requirement for protein was 120 grams. But besides this antiquated research factor, the Almighty dollar has seen it in its best interest to support that view. The huge economic interests of the billion-dollar livestock, dairy and meat-packing industries would not yield without a bitter fight any idea or research conclusion to the contrary that could jeopardize their business. In fact, through innumerable, clever and subtle advertisements, the doctrine has been diligently taught to the public for decades. The brainwashing job could hardly have been more thorough.

Fortunately, however, we now know where we can turn to, for reliable, unmanipulated information on the subject. Much research over the last few decades by these independent groups, shows that our daily protein requirement is far less than that which was formerly believed. Dr. D.M. Hegsted of Harvard University, found that 27 grams daily were sufficient for a person's needs. Dr. William C Rose's research has shown that about 20 grams of mixed proteins with about 66 percent being "complete," are quite adequate for optimum health.

Dr. Gagnar Berg, world-renowned Swedish nutritionist whose texts are used in many medical schools, after conducting extensive research on protein, was convinced that 30 grams of protein daily, were liberally adequate. His conclusion is shared by other outstanding scientists and nutritionists working independently. Dr. V.O. Siven Finnish scientist, believes the same—30 grams. Dr. Chittenden, American scientist conducting extensive experiments with soldiers and athletes, discovered that 30 to 50 grams of protein daily were adequate for the most strenuous physical performance. He demonstrated that, ironically, heavy taxing performance was better sustained on a low-protein diet.

Finally, both in Germany and Japan there are leading scientists whose research concludes that a low-protein diet is healthier. Dr. Kuratsune, Japanese researcher, has shown that 25 to 30 grams of protein daily, is quite enough for good health. Again, Dr. K. Elmer, German professor, experimenting with athletes, found that their performance significantly improved after they were switched from a daily regimen of 100 grams of animal protein to a regimen of 50 grams of vegetable protein.

So we can begin to see hopefully, that even though we have been thoroughly brainwashed into believing that we need "lots of proteins" by flesh-eating propagandists and businessmen, that the whole truth of the matter has not given to the American public. There is greater need for exposure on these issues to the international scientific community. Thus from the standpoint of the independent international scientific community, the recommendation is that a low-protein diet of about 30 to 50 grams of proteins daily (the variation needed to accommodate the needs of different individuals under varied circumstances), is quite adequate for vigorous and superior health.

HAZARDS OF A HIGH-PROTEIN DIET

This recommendation is greatly corroborated when we consider some of the problems generated by a diet that is excessively high in proteins. The general result of ingesting excess protein, is greatly increased toxemia in the system, with overall susceptibility to degenerative or other pathogenic disorders, as the immune system becomes progressively depressed with toxins.

Professor Kofrani of the already mentioned Max Plank Institute for Nutritional Research, observed that an excess of proteins only "builds more toxins." This is readily understood when it is remembered that excess proteins are not stored in the body, but broken down and utilized as energy or stored as body fat, producing at the same time some toxic by-products.

More specifically, not only are the tissues filled with toxic residues, but biochemical imbalances with excessive acidity result. Other resultant conditions are: accumulation of uric acid, urea and toxic purine in the tissues; reduced muscular strength and stamina, since the above-mentioned toxins inhibit proper nerve-muscle coordination and functioning, and also there is intestinal putrefaction which again provokes constipation with increased auto-toxemia as a result.

With increased putrefaction, there is poor intestinal micro flora which may result in B6, and B12 deficiency. And finally where the practice of eating excess proteins is chronic, there may ultimately be arteriosclerosis, heart disease and kidney damage. In fact even arthritis may develop. Dr. Gerber, professor at New York University, recently observed that "faulty protein metabolism" may be one of the contributory factors in the arthritis enigma. Thus, the hazards of excess proteins are very real indeed.

ANIMAL OR VEGETABLE PROTEIN—
WHICH IS SUPERIOR?

There are still other questions, however, to be considered with respect to the protein controversy. Which is really better, animal protein or vegetable protein as far as optimal human health is concerned? Is it possible to have vibrant, vigorous health without animal protein? Are meat-eaters healthier than vegetarians? Are all vegetable proteins incomplete? Do animal proteins have a higher biological value than vegetable proteins?

Once again in answering these questions we remember that much of the conflicting ideas and subjective opinions disguised as "scientific facts" that we have heard in the past, were attributable to the corrupting influence of commercialism (the omnipotent dollar) on research, also the lack of absolutely dependable, up-to-date research. Fortunately, however, we now have reliable scientific data to answer these questions. Evidence comes from international sources, as well as reliable research done right here in the United States. Once again Dr. Paavo Airola, world-renowned nutritionist of giant research and extensive experience in Europe, the U.S.A. and internationally, offers authoritative answers to these moot questions.

A scientific study conducted on a religious group living in the United States (Seventh-Day Adventists) and reported in the Journal of American Medical Association, convincingly elucidates the question as to whether flesh eaters have superior health to vegetarians, other factors being equal. This extraordinary study conducted by various medical doctors demonstrated that Seventh-day Adventists who for religious convictions do not eat flesh, possessed.

— 50% less dental caries among their children.

—400% less death rate from respiratory diseases.

—100% lower mortality rate from all causes.

—1000% reduced death rate from lung cancer.

Amazingly, this group of people, numbering more than a million, lives right here in the U.S.A., exposed to the same environmental and other stresses, like the general populace. These extraordinary statistics explode the fallacies, with which we have been brainwashed for decades. Really truth cannot be suppressed forever. The truly scientific principle or method, is for one (whether layman or expert) to be willing to modify or discard past theories or beliefs in the light of new and more reliable scientific research. Any other attitude must be described as academic dogmatism—the very evil that has suppressed, ignored or discredited valuable truth and data for centuries and kept back humanity from greater progress and enlightenment.

THE HEALTHIEST PEOPLE OF THE WORLD

Indeed these aforementioned statistics are perfectly consistent with extensive studies done on certain outstandingly long-lived races on the globe: notably the Bulgarians, Russians, Hunzas and others. Bulgarians, for instance, have been described as the tallest and most healthy people in Europe. Possessed of uncommon vigor and longevity, Bulgaria boasts more centenarians than any other country on planet earth. In contrast to about 10 centenarians per million of flesh-eating Americans, Bulgaria boasts 1,600 persons per million. Significantly, but consistently, these people utilize very little meat and most of the centenarians have been vegetarians (Airola 1971).

The Russians likewise have a health certificate comparable to that of Bulgarians, with seven times as many centenarians per million as the United States. Theirs is a low-protein diet, with the larger proportion of this being of vegetable proteins. Interestingly, most of the centenarians have been vegans (complete vegetarians using no animal products).

The Yemenite tribe of Semitic extraction and the Mayan Indians of Yucatan, similarly constitute evidence that meat-eaters are not healthier than people with a well-balanced vegetarian diet. While the Yemenites ate very little meat, the Mayans were total vegans whose staple diet consisted of vegetables, corn and beans.

Again, besides all the convincing cumulative evidence, the testimony of the Hunzas, adds even greater weight on the side of the scale in favor of a low-protein and /or vegetarian diet. While Bulgarians may be described as the healthiest people in Europe, the Hunzas have been considered as the "healthiest people in the world," by many researchers who have studied the secrets of their legendary longevity. Most of the frightful and common degenerative or killer-diseases of western civilization (heart disease, cancer, hypertension, arteriosclerosis, arthritis, diabetes, rheumatic disorders, etc.), are virtually unknown among these healthy people.

The health of us as Americans would appear in pitiful contrast next to these health veterans, who generally reach 90 to 100 and are astoundingly, still vigorous and virile at that age. Once again, as the researchers agree, the principal factor or secret of their health and longevity is their nutrition. It is high in natural complex carbohydrates and low in animal proteins. In fact, grains like buckwheat, barley and wheat plus apricots, apples, grapes and various vegetables with a little goat milk, constitute their stable diet.

Though up to this point it has been strongly implied, the question, "is animal protein better than vegetable protein?", could be more directly addressed. For decades we have been told that animal proteins were superior and indispensable to good health, and that vegetable proteins were inadequate to sustain health; that while animal proteins were "complete," having all the eight or nine essential amino-acids, vegetable proteins were not. The belief was that only meat, milk, eggs and fish contained complete proteins. However, again, recent scientific research on the international front has been exploding these myths that have been so thoroughly inculcated in our consciousness.

The Max Plank Institute in Germany, world-famous institution for nutritional research, alluded to, at various times previously, has made discoveries that disprove this erroneous view about vegetable proteins not being complete. Its research, corroborated by other research centers, has demonstrated that many vegetables, fruits, seeds, grains and nuts contain significant quantities of complete protein. For example, almonds, sesame and sunflower seeds, soybeans, potatoes, along with many fruits and green vegetables, possess complete proteins contrary to previous orthodox scientific belief.

Two other even more astounding discoveries in this connection, which Dr. Airola shares, are: 1) Vegetable proteins have a higher biological value than animal proteins, and that 2) Proteins in raw foods have a higher biological value than cooked proteins, so that you only need 50 percent of the normally- required amount of proteins if you eat raw vegetables, instead of cooked animal proteins. For the orthodox conventional mind this is perhaps so unexpected as to be considered incredible. Further, in the same Germany where 10 percent of the daily average protein intake is supplied by potatoes, it has been shown that potatoes possess proteins of superior quality. Shockingly, people have lived for as long as six years with potatoes as their only source of proteins and have enjoyed vigorous health.

Thus in summarizing the answers to the moot questions of the protein controversy, we have seen that a low-protein diet of between 30 and 50 grams per day, with emphasis on vegetable proteins, rather than animal proteins, and better still, consumed in as raw a state as possible, constitute a solid nutritional foundation upon which to build vibrant and vigorous health. Stated another way, a lacto-ovo vegetarian diet (diet including milk and eggs), drawn from a wide variety of foods, in as natural and raw a state as possible with emphasis on high quality complex carbohydrates and low proteins, is one of the most powerful nutritional secrets of superior health and extended longevity.

Truly it has been said that once orthodox scholasticism fought and persecuted Galileo for teaching that the world was round, when the conventional view was that it was flat, but their suppression of his ideas and persecution of him could not change truth into error. Truth is ultimately insuppressible, unconquerable.

ALKALI/ ACID CONSIDERATIONS

The human body works effectively to maintain a proper Ph. balance. Ph. is a measure of how alkaline (basic), or acidic a solution Isaiah. When a solution is neutral, that is, neither basic nor acidic, it is represented on the Ph. scale as 7. Ranging from this number to zero, is a measure of increasing acidity. Conversely, alkalinity increases as the Ph. rises from 7 to 14. Water which is neutral, is the medium in which chemical reactions take place, and helps in the maintenance of the Ph. balance. Normally the blood is slightly alkaline while urine is slightly acidic. Amid the multitudinous chemical reactions, and fluid interchanges in the system, the body normally maintains its constant Ph. equilibrium.

If conditions become too alkaline or acid in the system, death can result. Over-acidity (acidosis), in the body is especially dangerous to health, and is usually associated with diseases like arthritic and rheumatic disorders. Foods have a decided effect upon the body chemistry's acid-alkali equilibrium. Foods generally leave an acid, neutral or alkaline ash in the system after metabolism. That is, most foods are either alkali-forming or acid-forming. Understanding, identifying and utilizing these foods judiciously, and in proper proportions, can significantly enhance health.

When the body's supply of alkaline reserves is low or exhausted and enough alkali-forming foods are not consumed, acidosis is the natural consequence, since alkali neutralizes acids and vice versa. Research has shown that in a healthy body, there is a generous amount of alkali reserves in the tissues. These are used in the body to meet emergency demands when acid conditions begin to predominate or threaten to disrupt the proper balance.

Dr. Airola, consistent with reliable research, explains that the natural ratio in a normally healthy body is approximately 4 to 1. That is four parts alkali to 1 part acid or 80% to 20% He stresses that it is a vital and dynamic health principle to maintain this ratio in the diet as well. When this principle is consistently followed, the body's alkali reserves are plentiful and thus resistance to disease is greatly enhanced.

In other words, it is important for vigorous and superior health and vitality, to keep the diet slightly over-alkaline. The body can only function effectively with adequate alkaline reserves in the tissues. Diseases strengthen and thrive in acidosis conditions in the system. Interestingly, this balance seems automatically provided in a low protein diet. Vegetables and fruits generally (especially in their natural state), are alkali-forming, while seeds, nuts and grains are predominantly acid-forming. The body needs both of these classes of foods.

FOOD FOR THOUGHT

Did you know that for superior or optimum health that 80 % of your diet should consist of alkali-forming foods (essentially fruits and vegetables), and only 20% of acid-forming foods? To do otherwise is to commit slow suicide.

ACID-FORMING FOODS

barley	bread	beans
candy	cashew nuts	cereals
chestnuts	corn	chicken
corn products	cottage cheese	crackers
cream of wheat	eggs	flour, rye, wheat
fish	grapenuts	most grains
lentils	macaroni	maize
organ meats	oatmeal	oysters
peanuts	peanut butter	pecans
peas, dried	rice	sauerkraut
sugar	syrup	tapioca
walnuts	zwieback	

ALKALI-FORMING FOODS

alfalfa	alfalfa products	almonds
apples	apricots	artichokes
avocados	bananas	beans, lima, wax,
beans, kidney	beets	blackberries
blueberries	Brazilian nuts	broccoli
buttermilk	buckwheat	
broth, vegetable	cabbage	cantaloupe
carrots	cauliflower	celery
cherries	chicory	coconut
cranberries	cucumber	currants
dandelions	dates	eggplant
endive	figs	garlic
goat's milk	grapes	grapefruit
honey, pure	juice, fruit	juice, vegetable
kale	kelp	leek
lemons	lettuce	limes
milk	millet	muskmelon
okra	olives, ripe	olive oil
onions	oranges	oyster plant
parsley	parsnips	peaches
pears	peas, fresh	peppers, peppermint leaves
persimmons	pineapple	plums
potatoes	prunes	pumpkins
radishes	raisins	raspberries
romaine	rhubarb	rutabagas
savory	sorrel	soy beans
soy bean products	spinach	sprouts
squash	strawberries	Swiss chard
tomatoes	turnips	watercress
watermelons	wheat germ	

There are, of course, exceptions to rules. Millet and buckwheat, for instance, unlike most grains, are alkali-forming. Under conditions of sprouting, seeds and grains become less acid, and more alkaline. Chlorophyll-rich plant juices are extremely alkaline, as is fig juice.

FOOD FOR THOUGHT

Millet and buckwheat, unlike most grains, are alkali-forming. Under conditions of sprouting, seeds and grains become less acid, and more alkaline. Chlorophyll-rich plant juices are extremely alkaline, as is fig juice.

POWERFUL ENEMIES OF NUTRITION AND HEALTH

Unfortunately, not all that profess to be the healing arts are really true helpers to the body's healing faculties. Under the name of and auspices of medicine, there have been great abuses practiced upon diseased mankind and even in modern times this has been frequently done.

Ironically this is not only perpetrated by quacks, but by men of science who have set themselves up as the unchallenged experts and authorities in all matters of health and have even entrenched themselves legally to protect their monopoly. Lamentably, allopathic medicine in this country has not been (totally) free from the corrupting influence of commercialism—the almighty dollar—and this has definitely not been a blessing to the health of the masses.

The great explosion of knowledge of the sciences over the last century has created the illusion that medical science has really been making great progress in conquering disease. And while much technical information has been amassed and impressive surgeries can be performed today, generally, man is not gaining the upper hand in the battle with disease. The great increase in the number of doctors, hospitals, potent drugs, marvelous technology and billions expended, cannot keep pace with the grievous deluge of new and old diseases that threaten to overwhelm the planet.

As we look at modern allopathic medicine today there is reason for much concern. Instead of getting to the root-causes of diseases, modern medicine is content to treat symptoms and perform intricate and elaborate surgeries. While some of these treatments do have a place in emergencies and trauma, one cannot but be astonished at the fundamental dishonesty and absurdity of treating and suppressing symptoms with drugs, while giving people the false impression that they are being cured.

Drugs are today considered as the cornerstone of medicine. Whatever the diseases, whatever the causes, drugs are looked to for the answer, thus allopathic medicine has deliberately put a blind, as it were, upon its own eyes, so that they only look down the drug tunnel for answers and solutions to virtually all health problems. The real explanation for these practices, is the corrupting power of the Almighty dollar—the questionable marriage between the billion-dollar drug industries and the medical industry.

Toxic drugs constitute one of the most implacable enemies of nutrition and of nature's marvelously intricate healing faculties. While they alleviate, suppress and modify symptoms, by not reaching the real cause, the suppressed symptoms often resurface in more complex, deep-rooted and often fatal diseases.

What are some of the dangerous side effects of popular toxic drugs introduced into the system? In chapter three we already explored some of the baleful and horrible side effects of aspirin (acetylsalicylic acid), cortisone and gold injections. These drugs have been used extensively in the treatment of arthritis and acetylsalicylic is a popular pain-killer. Practitioners do not always tell patients about the toxic side effects of these drugs, and too often patients are used as guinea pigs. New drugs are made and declared "safe" by the authorities and marketed. However, after a few years or a decade as the horrible side effects become notorious, those drugs are discarded or shipped to third world countries and other newer drugs are advocated and declared "safe" for use. Thus, the vicious cycle is repeated.

Indomethacin, trimethylene-thiosphosphoramide, phenylbutazone, etc., are examples of the complicated, almost unpronounceable names that frequently disguise the insidiously toxic character of the substances. It would even appear that these incredible names mystify patients and further confirm their impressions that the beings who understand and use these mysterious chemicals must certainly not be ordinary men, and that these "potions" may indeed have mystical powers to heal disease. In short many doctors today influence clients in a way not unlike the way the medicine man awed his patients.

The list of toxic drugs with dangerous side effects that comprise the modern pharmacopeia today is virtually infinite. It would be a gargantuan task to enumerate and analyze them in their true nature, effects and scope. Suffice it to say that most of these drugs undermine the efforts of the body's own healing agencies, and open the door for more dangerous pathogenic complications and disorders with prolonged use. As I said earlier, drugs and surgery do have a place in certain traumatic or emergency situations, but oh that modern medicine, with respect to its almost exclusive drug use, would cure itself of its tunnel vision syndrome!; oh that it would not be so arrogantly intolerant of alternative forms of medicine that have been effectively used for millennia!

Other drugs too that people use for pleasure, likewise, significantly antagonize nutritional medicine: alcohol, cocaine, marijuana, heroin, PCB, tobacco, caffeine, etc., the list could be lengthy indeed. Of these, the use of alcohol is perhaps the most widespread. Though alcohol provides some calories, it cannot properly be considered a food. Many health experts, knowing that many people would have great difficulty in relinquishing alcohol use, advise using it in moderation. The truth is as E.G. White— an internationally-recognized educator observed: —"Moderate drinking is the school in which men train for a drunkard's career." The fact is that health is endangered by alcohol use even in "moderate" use, and brain cells begin to be affected and sometimes die.

Tobacco (nicotine) is an even more insidious drug than alcohol and a great health destroyer. It accounts for a large percentage of lung cancer, emphysema, unhealthy or deformed babies at birth, and lots of other nicotine-related health complications. Current research is showing that tobacco may even be implicated in leukemia.

- Processed, refined and canned foods.

- Coffee, tea, chocolate, cola and soft drinks.

- Unhealthy spices, MSG, black and white pepper, mustard, white pepper, rancid foods.

- Excessive use of salt and fat, especially saturated fat.

- Hurried eating, poor mastication, and drinking with meals which dilutes the digestive fluids, lowers the temperature of the stomach, and thus delays or impedes effective digestion.

- Refined white sugar, white flour and their products.

- Household and environmental toxic chemicals.

- Sedentary life styles.

- Worry, anxiety, stress and intemperance.

Most of these elements are commonly known to debilitate health. These harmful spices tend to irritate the digestive organs and inflame them. Processed and refined foods are generally robbed of vital nutrients, and though "enriched" or "fortified" with synthetic vitamins, all too frequently, sugar, salt and hazardous preservatives are added. Besides there is no laboratory superior to nature's. As previously discussed, excessive use of salt and fat (especially saturated fat), is implicated in hypertension in some cardiovascular disorders.

The value of exercise is unquestionable. Lack of exercise is indeed a serious enemy of health. A sedentary lifestyle induces a sluggish metabolism with accumulation of toxic waste products, tissue suffocation, and thus premature cellular degeneration, aging, and even heart attacks.

Exercise keeps the excretory organs working efficiently, enhances digestion and overall metabolism, as well as tones up the muscles. Vigorous exercise regularly in the open air improves cellular and tissue oxygenation and thus helps to keep them at maximum working efficiency.

Temperance is here defined as moderation in all the necessary functions of life and a careful abstinence from all harmful indulgences— avoid extremes, let moderation always be the key for the good and the pleasurable.

The baleful influence of stress upon human health, though generally recognized, cannot be over stressed. One can eat the healthiest diet in the world, yet if there are severe mental and emotional stresses, digestion and assimilation would be inhibited and health would deteriorate. In fact it has been found that stress can break down the system much faster than malnutrition.

Worry, fear, anger, tensions, hate, anxieties, envy, jealousy, feelings of being unloved, all negative emotions and attitudes can physiologically and psychosomatically provoke almost every class of diseases known to man. Hence, there is a need to shun stress as a most implacable enemy of good health and nutrition. We have already mentioned that the converse is likewise true. Positive emotions, trust and faith in God, relaxation and peace of mind are compatible and powerful allies of health and nutrition. They create a congenial biochemical environment in which nature can well perform her restorative functions.

DEALING WITH OBESITY

Of the many characteristic health disorders in the U.S.A., the link between nutrition and obesity is perhaps the most undeniable. It is an area that is extensively discussed and researched, but unfortunately, much controversy still surrounds the issues of causes and treatment. What is indisputable, however, is that it is a major health problem in this country with approximately 24 percent of women and 22 percent of men being obese.

A certain quantity of fat tissue is needed in the body for the accommodation of mechanical shock, for reserve energy and for insulation of the body from heat or cold. Adipose tissue also offers a measure of protection against environmental stresses. But obviously, too much adipose tissue is very hazardous to health. There is a distinction between obesity and overweight. Yet persons who are more than 20 percent overweight, are generally obese. There is disagreement as to what is ideal weight for height, frame and age, but individuals who are about 20 percent or less of the commonly-used tables of desirable weights may not necessarily be obese, since muscles and bones in some people may account for this difference. On the following page is a typical table of desirable weights for men and women.

What are the health risks associated with being over weight? The alarming fact is that there are many. They principally include the following:

- Accidents
  Hyperlipidemia

- Complications from surgery
  Poor quality life

- Diabetes
  Psychological problems

- Depression

- Skin disorders

- Gall bladder disease
  Shortened life span

- Gout
  Hypertension

- Varicose veins

- Complications from pregnancy
  Injury to weight-bearing joints

- Certain types of cancer
  Infertility

What are the causes of obesity? While it is the result of the ingestion of more food energy than is expended, the root causes that trigger this behavior are quite involved. Why do some people develop these compulsive habits to eat more than their bodies need? There are two theories propounded to account for this behavior. One is called the nature theory and the other the nurture theory. The nature theory is premised upon four points: 1) That obesity is linked to genetic traits passed down from parents. 2) Some animals are obese through their genes, the same may hold for humans. 3) Each person has a biologically determined weight. 4) There seems to be a difference in thermogenesis, from individual to individual, which difference is "natural."

The nurture theory on the other hand propounds that obesity stems essentially from 1) Habits of overeating developed in infancy, 2) Physical inactivity, 3) Psychological factors like boredom, 4) The constant accessibility of favorite foods and the presence of a greater number of fat cells due to overeating.

Both of these theories are plausible, the truth, however, is that combinations of both are likely to be the real root causes of the drive and behavior that are so very difficult to change. All the experts, nonetheless, agree that with regards to obesity an ounce of prevention is better than a pound of cure.

There are many fad diets that offer quick fixes for the problem of obesity, and in fact, many do stimulate a quick weight loss, sometimes even impressively, but almost invariable the weight goes up right back, after getting off the program and a vicious cycle is set in motion that gets progressively worse. Many of these fad diets are besides, nutritionally unbalanced and thus dangerous to overall health.

In treating the problem an understanding of the science of nutrition is an enormous advantage. While the psychological or behavioral factors may need professional attention, a knowledge of food values and properties can greatly help one identify and avoid the fat-promoting foods or combinations. Some invaluable tips are offered for overcoming the problem.

TIPS FOR CONQUERING OBESITY

* Eat slowly.
* Remove temptations and external eating cues.
* Increase daily physical activity.
* Plan alternate activities for when the temptation comes to eat.
* Have a diet plan; eat meals at regular times.
* Use much salad, fruits or high-fiber foods. They fill up without adding too many calories.
* Leave the table before feeling "full."
* As you shop, remember to avoid high-calorie / low-nutrient foods.
* When cooking, eliminate excess fat calories.
* When cooking, eliminate eating cues.
* Plan ahead for special occasions.
* Drink much water before to help feel full if need be, and
* Don't submit to social pressure to overindulge.
* Reduce fat calories even when dining out.

Indeed, your knowledge of nutrition will prove a great asset in the fight against obesity.

FOOD FOR THOUGHT

Wisen up! Ignorance will kill you and your loved ones. Know-ledge of nutrition can preserve your life and will prove a great asset in the fight against obesity.

TABLE OF DESIRABLE WEIGHTS FOR MEN AND WOMEN
25 YEARS AND ABOVE
(Weight in pounds with indoor clothes and shoes).

MEN

HEIGHT	LARGE FRAME	MEDIUM FRAME	SMALL FRAME
5'2"	126-141	118-129	112-120
5'3"	129-144	121-133	115-124
5'4"	132-148	124-136	118-126
5'5"	135-152	127-139	121-129
6"	138-156	130-143	124-133
7"	142-161	134-147	128-137
8"	147-166	138-152	132-151
9"	151-170	142-156	136-145
10"	155-174	146-160	140-150
11"	159-179	150-165	144-154
6'0"	164-184	154-170	148-158
1"	168-189	158-175	152-162
2"	173-194	162-180	156-167
3"	178-199	167-185	160-171
4"	182-204	172-190	164-175

TABLE OF DESIRABLE WEIGHTS FOR MEN AND WOMEN
25 YEARS AND ABOVE
(Weight in pounds with indoor clothes and shoes).

WOMEN

HEIGHT	LARGE FRAME	MEDIUM FRAME	SMALL FRAME
4'10"	104-119	96-107	922-98
11"	106-122	98-110	94-101
5'0"	109-125	101-113	96-104
1"	112-128	104-116	99-107
2"	115-131	107-119	102-110
3"	118-134	110-122	105-133
4"	121-138	113-126	108-116
5"	125-142	116-130	111-119
6"	129-146	120-135	114-123
7"	133-150	124-139	118-127
8"	137-154	128-143	122-131
9"	141-158	132-147	126-135
10"	145-163	136-151	130-140
11"	149-168	140-155	134-144
6'0"	153-173	144-159	138-148

PART THREE

BEING YOUR OWN DOCTOR AND OVERCOMING
HEALTH CONDITIONS

COMMON DISEASES
AND HERBS TRADITIONALLY USED FOR THEM

1. ANEMIA

HERBS USED

Alfalfa	Burdock	Chickweed
Dandelion	Kelp	Mullein
Nettle	Red Beet	Strawberry
Yellow Dock		

2. ARTHRITIS

An inflammation and painful soreness of the joints. Often there is even deformation of the bone structure which can become progressively worse. It is greatly aggravated by a diet high in animal proteins, fats and processed, refined foods.

DIETARY TIPS:
Use the Level two diet with emphasis on vegetables. Especially grated and eaten raw (pumpkin, potatoes, etc.). Liberally use watercress, alfalfa, celery, garlic, lemons and wheat grass, also, pineapples, sour apples and bananas. Goat's milk is also known to be very beneficial.

SPECIFICS:
* Raw potato juice therapy is especially good for arthritic and rheumatic conditions. Anciently the juice was made by taking a medium sized potato, and after washing it, cutting it with its skin into thin slices and putting them into a large glass of cold water. The water was then drunk on an empty stomach in the morning. If you have an electric juicer, make it fresh in the morning and dilute it with an equal quantity of water before drinking.
* Boil seven leaves from the sugarcane plant to obtain one large bottle of water. Use this during seven days (keep refrigerated, of course), and take a purge. Skip one week and then repeat. Do this for six months of necessary. You may then skip a month and begin the cycle again.

HERBS USED

Alfalfa	Burdock	Cayenne
Centaury	Chaparral	Comfrey
Horseradish	Horsetail	Lobelia
Parsley	Peppermint	Slippery Elm
Yucca		

3. BOILS/CARBUNCLES/ECZEMA

These occur when the body is full of impurities and poisonous wastes from bad-eating habits and poor elimination, also from stress and too little exercise.
* See IMPURE BLOOD and follow its program.
* Use Tonic formula #3, in this book for two weeks.
* Use sarsaparilla, red clover, nettle teas freely.
* Cabbage is excellent for skin disorders.
* Use beet and carrot juice, also other raw juices.

4. BRONCHITIS — SEE LUNGS

5. BURNS

HERBS USED

Aloes	Burdock	Chickweed
Comfrey	Hyssop	Marshmallow
Papaya	Plantain	Slippery Elm
St. Johnswort		

TIPS:
* Vitamin E, honey, egg white or aloe vera may be applied directly over burns. You can also add some white flour or ground oatmeal afterwards.
* Apply ice cold water and keep bandage wet and cold. Drinking a little cayenne will help if there is shock. Avoid aloe vera products that contain lanolin that may intensify the burns.
* Frequently applying fresh aloe vera gel is extremely effective for all burns, greatly speeding up the healing process.

6. CANCER/TUMORS

Cancer is a degenerative disease of modern civilization that is one of today's major killers. Numerous studies show that a wrong diet is one of the principal causes. Too much refined, processed, fragmented and over-cooked foods fill the system with toxins and waste substances that provoke cellular biochemical degeneracy and hence tumors, cancers and such like. Meat-eating, coupled with a sedentary and /or stressful life style is a primary contributor.

Research on groups like the Hunzakats, Navajo Indians and Seventh-day Adventists who do not eat meat show significantly less cancer among these people.

IF I HAD CANCER

I would use only natural medicine. I would not undergo the conventional approach of radical surgery, radiation or chemotherapy. Indeed they would only kill me faster as any really informed and honest doctor will admit if he has no money or selfish interest at stake. THE TOTAL APPROACH (Every true and natural biological method) is needed, but diet plays the major key. By effectively changing my diet and lifestyle with a sensible natural-oriented program, I would have reason to expect complete recovery if I follow my program consistently. I must also avoid all known pollutants or carcinogens.

DIETARY TIPS:

- A high-alkaline, non-flesh diet —See Dr. Stanford's Level One alkaline diet on page 101.
- An abundance of garlic, lemons, cabbage, broccoli, and raw pumpkin seeds.
- Bowel movement three times daily. See section on constipation.
- Hydrotherapy—especially sweat-inducing therapies like steam baths, cold water baths, saunas etc.
- Adequate exercise, rest, sunshine, fresh air and pure water are also of vital importance.
- Vitamins C, E, A, B-complex and beta-carotene as very good antioxidants, should be liberally used. Use foods naturally rich in them or natural supplements.

JUICES:

All green or dark colored juices, such as carrots, black cherries, red beets (from tops and roots), grape and black currants. Vegetable broths are also ideal.

NOTE:

It is of interest to note on passing that those clinics in Europe and elsewhere like the Ringber-Klink, in West Germany, that use nutrition (including raw foods) along with other biological therapies to treat cancer, boast a high rate of success.

CANCER /IMPURE BLOOD

Impure blood (toxemia) is the very foundation of most diseases. To cleanse, <u>follow the [3]level</u> two or level three alkaline diet for a month. Ensure that

[3]See Dr. Stanford's Three-Level Alkaline Diet.

the bowels move two to three times daily. (See constipation section). If you live in the West Indies or South America and cannot easily obtain the herbs listed for impure blood, you can take the charcoal/aloes treatment. See Tonic Formulas #3 on page.

HERBS USED

Aloes	Burdock	Buckthorn Bark
Cascara Sagrada	Chaparral	Comfrey,
Garlic	Ginger	Lobelia
Licorice root	Oregon Grape Root	Peach Bark
Prickly Ash Bark	Red Clover	Yellow Dock

7. CONSTIPATION

This is a serious cause of poor health. In fact, it is the root cause of most degenerative diseases. A wrong diet: too much protein, especially animal protein, processed and refined foods (too little fiber or roughage), drinking too little water, lack of exercise, bad food-combinations, worry and stress, etc. The bowels must be trained to move regularly. Do not delay unnecessarily when nature calls. This also provokes constipation.

TIPS:
- Boil a few senna leaves, strain and boil again with pitted prunes. Use a half teacup. Eat the boiled prunes.
- A tea of senna pods or leaves can be used alone. Since senna gripes, boil it with some ginger or peppermint.
- Avoid coffee, tea and alcohol, they are constipating beverages.
- Use ¼ teaspoon Epsom Salt in ½ to 1 teacup of pure water. You may use a teaspoon of honey.
- Avoid commercial laxatives. Use herbal laxatives instead.
- Avoid all refined, processed foods: sugar, white flour, white rice, white bread, etc.

HERBS USED

Aloe Vera	Barberry	Buckthorn
Bark	Cascara Sagrada	Chickweed
Dandelion	Flax Seeds	Mandrake
Olive	Peach Tree	Psyllium
Red Raspberry	Senna with Ginger	Slippery Elm
Tamarind	Turkey Rhubarb	

8. DANDRUFF

HERBS USED

Camomile	Chaparal	Sage
Yarrow		

- Eliminate all sugar from the diet. Avoid processed, refined foods.
- Castor oil alone, or in combination with olive oil, may be used on the hair effectively.

9. DIABETES

A common modern killer, it is caused chiefly by a wrong diet. That is a diet high in processed, refined carbohydrates, sugar, fat and grease. In short, a low-fiber, high-starch, or high sugar diet. Obesity and overeating are commonly involved. The pancreas breaks down in time and does not secrete enough insulin to process the starches and sugars and other carbohydrates in the body. Common symptoms include persistent thirst, frequent urination or the desire to urinate, persistent and excessive appetite. The three big giveaway keys: thirst, appetite and urine.

DIETARY TIPS:

- A Stanford [4]Level Two Alkaline Diet with emphasis on dark green leaves, bitter and sour herbs, fruits and vegetables. Sweet fruits can be used in moderation, because it is now known that insulin is not needed for the digestion of fruit sugar. Watercress is also good.
- Especially helpful are string beans, garlic, onions, celery, bora/bodi, egg plant, olives, lemons, apples, radishes.
- Calm the thirst with diluted fruit or vegetable juices, herb teas (use a little honey but not sugar), vegetable broths.
- Fasting is not advisable for diabetics, except under medical supervision.

HERBS USED

Alfalfa	Aloes	Cascara Sagrada
Cayenne	Celery	Comfrey Root
Dandelion Root	Ephedra	Eyebright
Golden Seal	Juniper Berries	Kelp
Nim	Parsley	Periwinkle
Raspberry Leaves	Most Bitter Herbs	

[4] See Dr. Stanford's Three Level Alkaline Diet

OTHER HELPS:
- Exercise is especially good for diabetics. So, take lots of exercise.
- Avoid constipation.
- Boil Mauby bark, refrigerate and use without sugar in its semi-bitter state. Boil the leaves of the nim tree. Take once per day for five days. Skip two days and repeat the cycle.
- Chew raw and swallow a few leaves and flowers of the periwinkle (white maid), or two nim leaves.
- Blend or grind up two or three cloves of garlic with a branch of celery. Drink a teacup on an empty stomach in the morning for six days. Skip one or two days and repeat.

10. DIARRHEA

Diarrhea may be caused by either parasites or metabolic disturbances due to digestive disorders.

TIPS:
- Use one teaspoon of activated charcoal or 3 tablets every two hours.
- Juice 2-3 lemons (diluting with water or herb tea) every 2-3 hours.
- Use white rice and/or grated apple. Peel the apples first.
- Pepsin or comfrey tablets.
- Papaya or banana is excellent for diarrhea.
- Carrot soup makes an excellent remedy for diarrhea as carrots help prevent digestive and intestinal problems and putrefaction.
- Drink 5 cups of herb tea made from one of the herbs listed for diarrhea.
- Use ½ teaspoon of nutmeg twice daily.
- For cramping, steep ½ teaspoon cloves in 1 quart of water and use periodically during the day.

HERBS USED

Cinnamon	Dried Blue Berries	Garlic	Ground Ivy
Guava		Peppermint	Periwinkle
Red Raspberry	Sage	Slippery Elm	
Sumac		White Oak Bark	

11. DIZZINESS—SEE ALSO HEADACHES

HERBS USED

Camomile	Catnip	Ginger
Hops	Peppermint	Valerian
Wood Betony		

12. EARACHES

* Cleanse the bowel—take an enema if necessary.
* Pour a few drops of garlic oil, mullein oil or lemon juice in the ear. An ice pack on the ear may help constrict blood vessels and relieve pain.
* Blend or chop a clove of garlic in the juice of two lemons or lime. Cover and leave for at least an hour, strain and pour a few drops in the ear. This may be used internally as well.
* Bake a whole onion, and when slightly warm, bandage around the ear.

13. EYE PROBLEMS

HERBS USED

Bayberry	Capsicum(cayenne)	Eyebright
Fennel	Golden seal	Plantain
Red raspberry		

* Two drops of castor oil, raw honey, or strained and diluted tea of Eyebright, capsicum, fennel, golden seal alone or combined may be used.
* These herb teas may be used internally and externally.

14. FEMALE PROBLEMS

These are principally caused or aggravated by wrong and artificial habits of living. A poor diet high in processed, refined and fragmented foods, too little exercise, constipation, smoking, alcohol, etc.

15. CRAMPS/DIFFICULTIES/MENSTRUATION

HERBS USED

Blue Cohosh	Catnip	Cayenne
Ginger	Hops	Parsley
Peppermint		

To Decrease Flow

Bayberry	Cayenne	False Unicorn
Golden Seal	Mistletoe	Plantain
Red Raspberry	White Oak Bark	

Suppressed Menstruation

Blue Cohosh	Camomile	Ginger
Parsley	Rue (small amounts)	Skullcap
Valerian		

OTHER HERBS USED

Garlic	Kelp	Passion flower
Wormwood		

- Dr. Stanford's Level two or three diet for 2-4 weeks.
- Follow the anti-constipation measures given.
- Get adequate exercise and rest; shun destructive habits like smoking, etc.
- Take a daily cold bath, which is very strengthening to the immune system and circulation, except during menstruation.

16. FIBROID— SEE TUMORS

17. FLU

- A liquid diet for 2-3 days (fruit juices, vegetable juices and/or broth, herbs teas with a little honey). Use no sugar. Pure sugarcane juice may be used.
- Blend 2-4 cloves of garlic in half a cup of lemon or lime juice. Cover and leave for at least one hour, then use a teaspoonful in some water or tea every hour or two.

HERBS USED

Alfalfa	Catnip	Cayenne
Fenugreek	Ginger	Golden Seal
Lemon grass	Peppermint	Red Clover
Red Raspberry	Rose Hips	Sage
Thyme	Yarrow	Slippery Elm

18. GUMS/MOUTH SORES/THRUSH/PYORRHEA

HERBS USED

Aloe Vera	Barberry	Bayberry Bark
Bistort	Black Walnut	Cayenne
Chickweed	Comfrey	Echinacea
Garlic	Golden Seal	Myrrh
Plantain	Red Raspberry	WhiteOak Bark
White Willow	Witch Hazel	

* A tea made from a combination of these herbs, especially from the ones in bold print, should be used. Keep in the mouth as long as possible before swallowing.
* Red raspberry is very good for cankers.
* Myrrh extract is also effective.
* White oak bark and golden seal or myrrh is a very powerful combination.

Vitamins: A, B-complex, E.
Minerals: Iron, magnesium, Phosphorous.

19. HALITOSIS *(Bad Breath)*

Though decayed dentures can cause bad breath, the primary and unsuspecting cause is digestive disturbances and constipation. Food ferments and putrefies in the intestines producing foul gases and toxins. These foul odors, especially when there is chronic constipation, pass into the bloodstream and then to the lungs and out through the breath during respiration.

HERBS USED

Garlic	Ginger	Golden Seal
Irish moss	Parsley	Peppermint
Rosemary	Wormwood	

* Use a raw food diet for a few days.
* Use wormwood tea (½ tbsp. to 1 cup water) for a week or two.
* Use nim or cascara sagrada or Swedish bitters.
* Eliminate animal proteins and dairy products from the diet for 1-3 months.
* Follow the anti-constipation program given in the book.
* Drink a cup of tea made of one of these herbs, 1 ½ to 2 hours after meals.

20. HEADACHES

Headaches are very characteristic of our fast-paced, overstimulated age. There are many causes, the principal of which is toxemia: an accumulation of poisonous waste in the system. Other causes include fatigue, over excitement, biliousness, indigestion, constipation, dehydration, high blood pressure, eye strain and disordered nerves, liver or body chemistry in general.

Migraine headaches, considered by some health authorities as tension headaches, may be caused by a deranged or rundown body chemistry, nerves and by a low blood sugar level. Headaches are symptoms of some underlying health problem and should not be ignored or brushed aside with an aspirin or commercial pain killer. They are warnings of the violations of health laws. While these measures may remove your awareness or feeling of pain— the health problem is still there and likely getting worse.

* Preservatives and Additives in food often cause headaches.

HERBS USED

Camomile	Catnip	Fenugreek
Ginger	Hops	Passion Flower
Peppermint	Skullcap	Thyme
Valerian	White Willow	

* Immersing or bathing the feet in very warm water with a cold towel around the head is a good remedy.
* Dip a cloth in hop tea and diluted apple cider vinegar, wring out and wrap around the head.
* Boil some water with equal parts of cider vinegar and inhale the vapor for a few minutes. In 20-30 minutes it should be gone.
* Put a tablespoon of Swedish bitter in water or tea (using one of the listed herbs) 2 or 3 times daily.
* Long term: eat sensibly and get enough rest, exercise and be temperate in all things.
* B-complex vitamins help much with headaches, especially migraines.
* Beware of Barbiturates, aspirins and like drugs which are very angerous.

21. HEART

The principal cause is faulty eating and/or obesity, along with unhealthy, stressful living habits. Animal proteins, with their high saturated fat content and high uric acid content, play a major role. Metabolic disorders like diabetes, obesity, smoking and lack of physical exercise complete the sad picture of America's number one killer disease. The risk factors must be eliminated for proper recovery.

HERBS USED

Barberry	Black Cohosh	Blue Cohosh
Cayenne	Chlorophyll	Garlic
Hawthorn Berries	Horsetail	Lobelia
Mistletoe	Oatstraw	Rose Hips
Safflower	Valerian	Wood Betony

* Follow the level two or three alkaline diet given in the book.
* To equalize blood pressure and thus relieve the heart, use a combination of cayenne, garlic, ginger (also ginseng and/or golden seal if possible), and parsley.
* For high blood pressure use cayenne and garlic.
* To strengthen the heart, use cayenne, garlic, hawthorn
* Do not overeat. Don't use coffee, animal flesh or animal fat, alcohol, tobacco, sugar or refined, processed, fragmented foods.
* Use very little salt. Use none for the first 2 weeks.
* Avoid distilled water which is deficient in minerals. Natural, unpolluted spring water is best.
* Do not use chlorinated water. Chlorine destroys vitamin E. Which is very essential for the heart.
* Get plenty of regular exercises.

22. HEMORRHAGE

Generally you may use any of the good astringent herbs listed below.

HERBS USED

Plantain	Bayberry	White oak bark
Cayenne	Bistort	Golden seal
Red raspberry	Slippery elm	Mullein
Comfrey	Nettle	

* Putting ice on a bleeding wound also helps contain bleeding.
* Lemon or lime juice may be snuffed up the nose to stop nosebleeding.

23. HEMORRHOIDS *(Piles)*

* Piles are caused chiefly by wrong diet and constipation.

* Follow the program outlined for constipation.
* Cut a piece of raw potato (red one best), about the size of your little finger and apply vitamin E (or olive as a substitute). Insert this into the rectum at nights. You may put charcoal powder on the cut potato with the vitamin E or olive oil for better effect.
* Charcoal and cocoa butter or fat or Vaseline may be used also.
* An enema made with the tea of an astringent herb like white oak bark, plantain (or even lemon juice, charcoal or garlic). Use 1 Tbsp. of the herb to 1 quart of water.
* Hot and cold sitz baths can help greatly.
* Simmer garlic powder and coca butter (or beeswax) Make into suppositories.

Insert one at bedtime and after each bowel movement.

24. HYPERTENSION *(High Blood Pressure)*

This common affliction today has several causes: principally a stressful life style with a wrong diet — too much salt, sugar, fat, spices, animal proteins and refined, processed foods. There may also be lack of exercise and a hereditary predisposition. More frequently, there are hereditary eating patterns. SYMPTOMS include headaches, often in the morning, dizziness, breathing difficulty, flushed complexion and blurred vision. These latter are also often seen in heart attacks, which again can be caused by high blood pressure.

Dietary Tips:
Use the level one or two diet with emphasis on garlic, oatmeal, lemons, onions, high-fiber foods.

HERBS USED

Cayenne	Golden Seal	Hawthorn Berries
Mistletoe Leaves	Valerian Root	Wild Cherry Bark

Tips:
* Get lots of exercise.
* Avoid undue stress.
* Have a dry brush massage once or twice daily.

25. HYPOGLYCEMIA *(Low Blood Sugar)*

HERBS USED
FORMULA # 1: Dandelion, horseradish, licorice, safflower.
FORMULA # 2: Cayenne, red clover, soybeans.

* Cleanse the glands, enhance digestion and circulation and fortify the nerves.
* Use the level two or three alkaline diet for a while.
* It is not necessary even with hypoglycemia to eat many meals daily like some doctors recommend. Nutritious fruit and/or vegetable juices can be taken between meals that will keep up the blood sugar level without over taxing the digestive system.

26. IMPURE BLOOD

Impure blood (toxemia) is the very foundation of most diseases. To cleanse, follow the level two or level three alkaline diet for a month. Ensure that the bowels move two to three times daily. (See constipation section). If you live in the West Indies or South America and cannot easily obtain the herbs listed for impure blood, you can take the charcoal/aloes treatment. See Tonic Formulas #3.

HERBS USED

Aloes	Burdock	Buckthorn Bark
Cascara Sagrada	Chaparral	Comfrey
Garlic	Ginger	Lobelia
Licorice root	Oregon Grape Root	Peach Bark
Prickly Ash Bark	Red Clover	Yellow Dock

27. INFECTIONS

These are Invasions of the body by microbes often characterized by in-flammation, swelling, etc.

HERBS USED

Black Walnut	Capsicum	Ginger
Echinacea	Garlic	Golden Seal
Lemons	Lobelia	Myrrh
Plantain	Watercress	Wormwood
Yarrow		

Tips:
* Vitamins A, B-complex, C, E.
* Minerals: zinc
* Garlic, charcoal or herb tea enemas.
* Garlic oil is a powerful medicine for infection, internally as well as externally.
* Watercress crushed or juiced is even more powerful than penicillin

28. INSOMNIA

Frequently caused by overstimulation: overwork, overeating, lack of exercise, worry and stress as well as eating too late and too heavy at night.

* A hot or warm footbath followed by a hot cup of tea made from leaves of calabash, sour sop and lettuce.
* Make a cup of herb tea from passion flowers.
* See HEADACHES. The same measure will induce sleep.
* A tea from hops is especially effective also.

29. JAUNDICE- See gallbladder

Follow treatment for gallbladder, diabetes, digestive disorders. Use bitter herbs, golden seal, garlic and lemons freely. A raw food diet for 2—4 weeks is indicated. During acute stages fomentation to the liver and stomach help greatly with pain.

30. KIDNEYS/BLADDER PROBLEMS

HERBS USED

Buchu	Comfrey	Corn silk
Cucumber	Dandelion	Golden seal
Juniper berries	Marshmallow	Nettle
Parsley	Slippery elm	Uva ursi
White oak bark		

Other Uses:
* Good also for Bed Wetting, Bloody Urine, Kidney Stones, Water Retention
* Formula 1: Camomile, dandelion, juniper, parsley, uva ursi
* Formula 2: Ginger, golden seal, juniper, lobelia, marshmallow, parsley, uva ursi.

31. KIDNEY STONES

* To pass kidney stones, take 2 tablespoons of lemon juice in water with one of the two herbal formulas given above every 30 minutes. This will also alleviate the pain.

32. WEAK BLADDER

* Eat 1 dozen raw pumpkin seeds daily for a few weeks.
* Boil the hairy tassel or beard found on corns, drink one or two cups daily for a month.
* Make slices of young green sour sop with skin, boiling the fruits and seeds—take twice daily until condition is overcome.
* Eating watermelon seeds helps young children urinate when they cannot.
* Eating the heart of the ripe soursop strengthens weak bladders in young children.

33. BED WETTING

* Use a tea made from cinnamon bark, or better, chew the bark.
* Give a spoon of honey just before bedtime.

34. LOW BLOOD PRESSURE

Often caused by a lack of vitality, a poor or poorly-assimilated diet, lack of exercise, etc.

Tips:
* Have a more nourishing alkaline diet 3level two or three.
* Take three pints of Welch's Grape Juice, or make your own, for a 6-day treatment. Swizzle a ½ pint with an egg [6](only from hens naturally bred without drugs). Take adequate rest and a nourishing diet. Orange juice may be substituted for grape juice, but the grape is better.

* Use the nut-milk tonic formula given in this book.

HERBS USED

Anise	Cayenne	Garlic
Ginseng	Hawthorn	Hyssop
Parsley	Rosemary	Shepherd's Purse
Yarrow		

---

[6]About 6-8 almonds may be substituted in place of the egg.

35. LUNG PROBLEMS/PNEUMONIA, EMPHYSEMA/PLEURISY

<u>HERBS USED</u>

Bayberry	Burdock	Cayenne
Chickweed	Comfrey	Eucalyptus
Fenugreek	Garlic	Ginger
Ginseng	Horseradish	Hyssop
Irish Moss	Licorice	Mullein
Pennyroyal	Plantain	Pleurisy Root
Rose Hips	Sage	Yarrow

* Use lemons, garlic and cayenne in liberal doses daily.
* Fennel, rose hips and garlic are ideal for emphysema or a combination of comfrey and fenugreek.
* For pleurisy, mix ½ teaspoon cayenne, 1 tablespoon lobelia, 3 table spoons slippery elm in water and use as a pack for one hour.
* Garlic oil rubbed well into the chest area is very effective.
* Follow the level two or three alkaline diet until recovery.

36. MEMORY/ENERGY/SENILITY/STERILITY/VITALITY

HERBS USED

Bayberry	Black Walnut	Cayenne
Comfrey	Dandelion	Don Qua
Echinacea	Ginseng	Gingko
Golden Seal	Gotu Kola	Hawthorn
Ho-shou-wo	Lemon Grass	Licorice
Myrrh	Peppermint	Safflower

37. MORNING SICKNESS/NAUSEA/VOMITING

HERBS USED

Alfalfa	Catnip	Eucalyptus
Fennel	Ginger	Hops
Kelp	Peach Leaves	Red Raspberry
Sage	Spearmint	Wild Yam

* The oil of some of these herbs can be used in various combinations for nausea.

38. NERVE PROBLEMS

These constitute another sign of our fast-paced, stress and tension-filled, modern society. Poor and weak nerves are a result of faulty eating and living habits. Poor elimination, excess worry, anxiety, lack of exercise, inadequate rest and sleep, excesses and overstimulation of the senses, are all culpable and injurious factors that must be removed for proper recovery of nervous health.

HERBS USED

Black Cohosh	Blue Cohosh	Camomile
Cascara Sagrada	Catnip	Celery
Fennel	Ginger	Golden Seal
Hops	Hyssop	Lobelia
Mistletoe	Passion Flower	Peach Leaves
Peppermint	Red Clover	Sage
Skullcap	St. Johnswort	Valerian
Wild Yam	Yarrow	Yellow Dock

* Eliminate the injurious factors that produce weak nerves.
* Eliminate hot spices from the diet except cayenne in moderation.
* Use yellow dock, cayenne and eucalyptus for nervous disorders.
* Follow the level two or three alkaline diet for a while.

39. NIGHT SWEAT

HERBS USED

Hops	Hyssop	Nettle
Sage	Strawberry Leaves	Yarrow

40. NIGHTMARES

HERBS USED

Hops	Lobelia	Peppermint
Skullcap	Thyme	Valerian
Wild Lettuce		

* Do not eat a heavy evening meal. Eat several hours before bed time.
* Take more vitamin B-complex, calcium and iron.
* Follow level three diet for a while.

41. OBESITY

While there is often a hereditary factor, faulty eating patterns are also inherited and are more often the real culprits for obesity. Eating habits must be changed, and a too sedentary lifestyle. Avoid sugar, refined, starchy, fragmented foods, fats, grease and much salt.

* Follow the level two or three alkaline diet for a while, depending on how fast the results are desired.
* Exercise must be a vital part of your lifestyle. Walking is an excellent exercise.
* Use the Papaya treatment: Take 10 papaya seeds daily as if they were tablets, with grapefruit peel tea. Boil the peel for 10 minutes to make the tea. Take this for 2 weeks, then skip 2 weeks and repeat. This can be followed with regular but sensible diet. — Take a fruit diet for one or two weeks for express results.
* Use the tonic formula #3 in the back of the book for a few weeks.

HERBS USED

Alfalfa	Black Walnut	Sea wrack
Burdock	Capsicum	Cascara Sagrada
Chickweed	Dandelion	Echinacea
Saffron	Fennel	Gotu Kola
Hawthorn	Horsetail	Kelp
Papaya	Parsley	Psyllium
Safflower	Sarsaparilla	Senna
Slippery Elm	Watercress	

Vitamins-
Multivitamins, B-complex, (B6, B12), inositol, E.

Minerals-
Calcium, magnesium, potassium, zinc.

Supplements-
Bee Pollen, Flaxseed, Apple Cider Vinegar, Kelp, Lecithin, Spirulina

42. UNDERWEIGHT

* Use calamus tea (Soak 1 teaspoon in ½ pint cold water for 12 hours, then heat gently, strain and drink slowly when cool).

* Use cornmeal porridge daily for a few weeks.
* Fenugreek in soy milk is very nourishing and builds weight.

43. PAIN—*See Headaches*

Pain is not a disease, but a symptom of some underlying health problem. Though aspirin is widely used, it is a dangerous drug. Its correct name is acetylsalicylic acid, a product of coal tar. Hiding the pain with aspirins or such like gives as false sense of security. Much better discover and remove the cause of deteriorating health. Aspirins can also cause ulcers.

HERBS USED

Camomile	Catnip	Corn Silk
Hops	Lobelia	Peppermint
Poke Weed	Primrose	Skullcap
Taheebo	Valerian	White Willow
Wild Lettuce	Wild Yam	Wormwood

44. PARASITE/WORMS

HERBS USED

Aloe Vera	Black Walnut	Garlic	Hops
Male Fern	Onion	Papaya Seeds	
Pumpkin Seeds	Sage	Slippery Elm.	
Valerian	White Oak Bark	Wormwood	

* Small children can eat pumpkin seeds and drink camomile, or worm wood tea.
* A week's treatment of charcoal, aloes and molasses (in the proportion of 2:3:1 teaspoons respectively) per day.
* Table salt for pin worms in children (heavy salt diet for 1 week).
* Take 1 tablespoon of fresh papaya seeds, chew and swallow on an empty stomach. A little honey may be added. Repeat several times. Dried papaya seeds can also be used. Blend with a little water, if necesary.

45. POISONING

* Charcoal is a very effective and harmless remedy for most types of poisoning. Use 2-4 tablespoons depending on the quantity ingested or severity.

Blood Poisoning

Charcoal	Chickweed	Echinacea
Plantain		

Food Poisoning

Charcoal	Chickweed	Lobelia
Slippery Elm		

46. PROSTATE PROBLEMS

After middle age this male sex gland often gives problems, but these can be overcome.

* Follow the level two or three alkaline diet for a while.
* The fat soluble vitamins (A, D, E, K) are very helpful for the condition.
* A hot sitz bath (105—115 degrees) soaking the pelvic region for 30 — 60 minutes is a very effective therapy.
* Avoid sexual excesses. Avoid undue prolongation of the sexual act which puts an undue strain upon the organ. Likewise avoid heavy sexual stimulation without a climax since the glands are engorged without re lease.
* Use zinc-rich food(brewer's yeast, onions, rice bran, nuts and seeds, molasses, peas, beans, wheat germs).
* Drink ½ teaspoon powdered slippery elm bark. Mix it with warm water without lumps and drink half glass warm water twice daily. This is very effective in acute pain.
* Pumpkin seeds are very effective for the condition.
* A simple and effective prostate massage consists in the following: Lie flat on the back, pull the knees up as far as possible then press the soles of both feet together, lower the legs as far as possible with a forceful movement. Repeat as often as possible.
* Walking is a highly recommended exercise for the condition.
* Smoking and alcohol must be abandoned.

HERBS USED

Blue Flag	Buchu	Corn Silk
Damiana	Echinacea	Garlic
Ginseng	Golden Seal	Juniper Berry
Kelp	Parsley	Peach Tree Leaves
Queen of the Meadow	Slippery Elm	Uva Ursi

47. RINGWORM

* Sealing off the air is effective for stopping fungoid parasites.
* Use garlic oil— internally and externally

* Apply every few hours a mixture of lemon juice, egg white and nail varnish.
* Apply tincture of lobelia and olive oil.

HERBS USED -

Black Walnut	Garlic	Golden Seal
Myrrh	Sarsaparilla	Taheebo
White Oak Bark		

48. SEX REJUVENATION/IMPOTENCE/MENOPAUSE-STERILITY

HERBS USED

Capsicum	Chickweed	Damiana
Dandelion	Echinacea	Garlic
Golden Seal	Gotu Kola	Pumpkin seeds
Sarsaparilla	Saw Palmetto	Siberian Ginseng

* Zinc is also beneficial.
* Smoking and alcohol must be given up. They debilitate the sexual system and the body.

49. SHOCK

HERBS USED

Cayenne	Ginger	Lobelia
Myrrh		Valerian

50. SICKLE CELL

Sickle cell anemia is where the cells of the white corpuscles are destroying or consuming the red corpuscles.
* Cleanse the body and build up the immune system.
* Follow the level two or three alkaline diet for a while.
* Increase the intake of zinc, along with vitamins C and E.
* Liberally use the juices of carrots, cauliflower, cabbage, and other green vegetables.
* See and follow the "Tonic formula #3" for two weeks.
* Drink a tea made of the leaves of the avocado pear.

51. SINUS/HEAD COLDS

Usually caused by wrong diet, wrong, mucus-forming food combinations, animal and dairy products, refined processed foods, etc. It is an accumulation of toxemia and mucous in the system and especially in the head.

Tips:
* Use a raw food diet of fruits and/or vegetable salads for 4-10 days (The longer the better).
* Avoid all refined, processed foods for one or two months.
* Use no animal or dairy products (except honey) for one to two months.
* Do not drink with your meals. Chew foods thoroughly.
* Use lemons and garlic abundantly. The powder of golden seal, bay berry, or Brigham tea may be snuffed up the nose. Alternatively, use a tea made from them. Method: Boil 1 pint of water with 1 teaspoon salt, 1 teaspoon soda and 1 teaspoon witch hazel. Use this liquid to snuff up the nose several times daily.
* Avoid constipation; let the bowels move 3 times daily.

<u>HERBS USED</u>

Aloes	Bayberry	Cayenne(bird pepper)
Comfrey	Eucalyptus	Garlic
Ginger	Golden Seal	Mullein
Rose Hips	Witch Hazel	

52. SKIN PROBLEMS/ACNE/ITCH

These usually result from a lot of accumulated toxins in the system due to a poor and faulty diet and constipation or poor elimination.

* See IMPURE BLOOD and CONSTIPATION on page .
* Follow a level two or three alkaline diet.

HERBS USED

Aloe Vera	Barberry	Bistort
Black Cohosh	Black Walnut	Brigham Tea
Buckthorn	Burdock	Calendula
Chaparral	Chickweed	Comfrey
Dandelion	Don Qua	Ginger
Golden Seal	Gotu Kola	Horseradish
Hyssop	Kelp	Mullein

Pennyroyal	Poke Weed	Red Clover
Safflower	Sage	Sarsaparilla
St. Johnswort	Taheebo	Thyme
White Oak Bark	Wintergreen	Yarrow
Yellow Dock -	Yucca	

* Ginger baths and poultices of Redmond Clay are very effective.
* Increase intake of vitamins A, B, C, F, P, Biotin, Niacin PABA, Riboflavin.
* Increase intake of the minerals: Iron, Silicon, Sulphur.

53. SPLEEN

HERBS USED

Barberry	Camomile	Cascara Sagrada
Cayenne	Dandelion	Golden Seal
Horseradish	Parsley	Uva Ursi
Yarrow	Yellow Dock	

54. SMOKING/COFFEE/ALCOHOL/DRUG ADDICTION

There is a physiological dependence brought about in the body by the prolonged abuse of any drug poison like is found in tobacco, coffee, alcohol or other drug. The body accustoms itself to a high level of the poison in the blood. When this level begins to decrease the body triggers a "hunger" or "craving" for it.

The key to breaking this physiological dependence is the thorough cleansing of the blood of these accumulated toxins. With juice fasting (an entirely liquid diet of fruit juices, vegetable juices, vegetable broths and/or herb teas). The body will effectually rid itself of these toxins. When the tissues, cells and blood are cleansed of the poison, the "craving" will be gone. Only a small amount of psychological dependence will remain a few months longer, but will eventually disappear.

See Lemon Cleanse Therapy on page under MASTER FORMULAS. This is highly beneficial for these conditions.

HERBS USED

Black Cohosh	Blue Cohosh	Catnip
Hops	Peppermint	Skullcap
Slippery Elm	Valerian	

* The herbs in bold, along with slippery elm removes the craving for tobacco.
* With juice fasting the craving is more quickly removed.
* Women who smoke age twice as fast as those who don't.
* Two (2) daily enemas must accompany juice fasting to eliminate toxins.
* Follow a level two or three alkaline diet afterward to build up your body and consolidate the great health victory.

55. SORE THROAT

HERBS USED

Bayberry	Cayenne	Chlorophyll
Comfrey	Eucalyptus	Fenugreek
Garlic	Golden Seal	Horehound
Hyssop	Licorice	Mullein
Myrrh	Pennyroyal	Pineapple
Red Raspberry	Rose Hips	Sage
Slippery Elm	Thyme White	Oak Bark
Witch Hazel	Yarrow	

* Use any of the above herbs (especially those in bold) to gargle the throat.
* Garlic and/or charcoal enemas fight infection.
* Gargling with salt water is also very effective.
* Dip a cloth or towel in salt water, wring it out and apply around the neck during night. Place a plastic over the towel to keep the pillow dry.

56. STOMACH /DIGESTIVE DISORDERS

HERBS USED

Alfalfa	Aloe Vera	Bayberry
Camomile	Cayenne	Dandelion
Eyebright	Fennel	Garlic
Ginger	Ginseng	Golden Seal
Hops	Lemon Grass	Myrrh
Papaya	Peppermint	Red Raspberry
Slippery Elm	Thyme	White Oak Bark
Wormwood		

* Using papaya or aloes with meals, helps digestion.
* Lemons and garlic, cayenne and 1 tablespoon olive oil are effective eaten with salads.

* One or two tablespoons of charcoal dissolved in warm water or herb tea is effective for almost any acute stomach problem.
* Okra, papaya and slippery elm, are good demulcents. Any one of them is excellent for stomach problems.

57. STRESS— *see Nerves*

58. TINNITUS

This is the condition of ringing in the ears. Hypoglycemia or hypertension can cause this as well as nutritional and chemical imbalances.

* See section dealing with HYPOGLYCEMIA and HYPERTENSION
* Follow the level two or three alkaline diet for a while.

HERBS USED

Alfalfa	Black Cohosh	Black Walnut
Buchu	Burdock	Capsicum
Chaparral	Corn Silk	Dandelion
Echinacea	Garlic	Ginger
Ginseng	Golden Seal	Gotu Kola
Hawthorn	Ho-shou-wu	Hops
Horsetail	Juniper Berries	Lady 's Slipper
Lobelia	Parsley	Red Clover
Skullcap	Valerian	Wood Betony

59. TONSILLITIS

HERBS USED

Aloe Vera	Burdock	Cayenne
Chlorophyll	Comfrey	Echinacea
Garlic	Golden Seal	Rose Hips
Sage	Slippery Elm	White Oak Bark

60. ULCERS (STOMACH)

* Eliminate everything that can irritate the mucus membranes of the stomach or duodenum.
* Chew foods thoroughly or use a blender. Salivate food well.
* A diet of papaya, banana, oatmeal, boiled potatoes, pumpkins/squash and such like, (or even white rice for a few days), is indicated.

- Use no fried foods, vinegar, mustard, black pepper, coffee, tea, salt, sugar, chilli, and similar hot spices. Cayenne may be used in moderation.
- When ulcers are present, the system needs to be properly cleansed. To this end, brush the skin to open the pores and strengthen the mucus membranes.
- Lemon juice diluted in water or herb tea is good for the condition. Start with small amounts and gradually increase.
- Milk from blanched almonds or goat's milk is beneficial.
- Avoid food or drink that is too hot or too cold. Avoid drinking with meals.
- Cabbage and/or potato juice is very effective for duodenal and stomach ulcers respectively. The juice must be made fresh as oxidation will quickly destroy the medicinal virtues.
- A tablespoon of charcoal, aloe vera, lemon juice and olive oil may be used.

HERBS USED

Alfalfa	Camomile	Canagra
Cayenne	Cloves	Comfrey Root
Flaxseed	Garlic	Golden Seal
Myrrh	Plantain	Slippery Elm
Violet	White Oak Bark	Yarrow

- A good herbal combination is golden seal, cayenne, and myrrh.
- Avoid undue stresses, irritations, worry and fret. Get enough exercise. Walking is one of the best and most natural of all exercises.

61. VARICOSE VEINS

Varicose veins usually result from stagnation of blood in the veins and consequent weakening of the blood-vessel walls and valves. Pregnancy, lack of exercise, obesity, constipation, and poor diet, are all contributory factors. Hemorrhoids are caused by enlarged veins around the anus. Blood vessels that become weak in the rectal area if allowed to worsen, can cause prolapsus of the anal wall, rupturing the veins and provoking infection. Prolonged standing is definitely not recommended. Brisk and regular walking is excellent for the condition.

- Follow the level two or three alkaline diet for a while.
- Avoid constipation studiously.
- Bathe and massage feet (or whole body) with cold water in the mornings. Rub with some apple cider vinegar afterwards.

HERBS USED

Bayberry	Cayenne	Witch Hazel
White Oak Bark		

* These herbs may be used internally as well as externally.

62. VENEREAL DISEASES

Sexually transmitted diseases are very current in today's promiscuous society. The main ones are Syphilis, gonorrhea and aids (HIV).

* Follow level one or two alkaline diet for a while.

HERBS USED

Aloes	Black Walnut	Buchu
Burdock	Echinacea	Garlic
Gentian	Golden Seal	Kelp
Oatstraw	Pau D'arco	Queen of the Meadow
Red Clover	Slippery Elm	Sumac
Taheebo	Uva Ursi	White Oak Bark
Witch Hazel	Yarrow	Yellow Dock

* Use the herbs internally as well as in the form of tea, externally for wash or douche. 1 tablespoon of charcoal in the wash or douche is also effective.
* 1 teaspoon of Swedish bitters drunk 2 or 3 times daily and also in douche or wash is very effective.

63. WARTS

* Castor oil applied liberally over the area morning and evening for a few months.
* Vitamin E from 1 capsule on a band-aid without medication and applied.
* Increase the intake of vitamins A and E.
* Cut raw potato and rub it on several times daily for 1 or 2 months.
* Apply the juice of green papaya several times daily or the juice of almost ripe figs for 1 or 2 months. The juice of celandine is also effective.

64. WATER RETENTION

HERBS USED

Blue Cohosh	Burdock	Catnip
Dandelion	Fennel	Fenugreek
Golden Seal	Gotu Kola	Hawthorn
Hops	Horsetail	Juniper
Parsley	Peach Bark	Safflower
Slippery Elm	St. Johnswort	Taheebo
Uva Ursi	Yarrow	

* Increase intake of vitamins B, and C.
* Increase intake of calcium and potassium.

65. YEAST INFECTION/VAGINAL PROBLEMS

HERBS USED

Aloe Vera	Barberry	Bistort
Black Walnut	Blessed Thistle	Blue Cohosh
Comfrey	Echinacea	False Unicorn
Fenugreek	Garlic	Ginger
Golden Seal	Horsetail	Marshmallow
Myrrh	Nettle	Plantain
Queen of the Meadow	Red Raspberry	Slippery Elm
Thyme	Uva Ursi	White Oak Bark
Wintergreen	Witch Hazel	

* Cleanse the body and intestines and seek to build the immune system.
* Follow the level two or three alkaline diet for a while.
* Use a douche of the herbs in bold, either alone or in combination. A good combination is aloe vera, white oak bark, garlic and cayenne. Horsetail can also be added.
* A douche of white oak bark or Bistort is good for vaginal bleeding.
* A tea of marshmallow, slippery elm or other demulcent herb is good for vaginal irritation.
* A tablespoon of powdered charcoal dissolved in garlic water or herb tea also makes a good douche.
* A douche of fresh garlic, aloes and white oak bark or charcoal should clear up yeast infection in three days.
* Insert home made yogurt into the vagina.
* For babies or young children, rub area with garlic oil or wash it with garlic water.

DR. STANFORD'S
THREE-LEVEL ALKALINE DIET

Level One Alkaline Diet

This diet is classified as the EMERGENCY DIET and is indicated for critical illness. It is the most powerful of the three and offers the greatest potential for the fastest recovery of health. It also represents the highest or strictest level of dietary discipline of the three. It comprises three phases, like the others, but of differing lengths of time.

PHASE ONE
FIRST 30 DAYS DURATION
(From day 1 to day 30)

- 100% ALKALINE DIET (can with great benefit also extend for an other month)
- A mono (short for monotrophic) diet (a single kind of food article at a meal) is best. That is, use grapes only ideally (for three meals daily — use the quantity and variety that you desire) for 2-4 weeks. This holds extraordinary cleansing and healing potentials. This is the number one recommendation for those who have the discipline. Grapes, papaya, pineapples, oranges, mangoes, or bananas can also be used with respectively increasing therapeutic and cleansing merit from right to left. In other words, grapes would be the best choice if you can get them, papaya second, etc.

- 100% Uncooked foods: (fruits or raw vegetable salads), is the alternative to, or second choice in place of the mono diet. This should be followed for the rest of phase one, after your mono diet terminates.
    Observe the contraindications given in this section strictly. No harmful foods whatsoever!

PHASE TWO
NEXT 60 DAYS DURATION
(From day 31 to 90)

- Only a small potion (5-10%) of steamed or lightly-cooked foods may be used.
- The diet should consist of 85% alkaline-forming foods and only 15% acid-forming foods.
- Keep observing your contraindications. Do not fall back.

PHASE THREE
NEXT UMPTEEN DAYS
(From day 91 to indefinite)
+ Use 80% alkaline-forming foods and 20% acid-forming foods. See the table on acid and alkali-forming foods on page.
+ Eat sensibly and watch those harmful foods. It costs too much to be sick again.
+ Keep the emphasis on raw foods (the greater part). Remember there are marvelous healing and cleansing properties in raw foods.

FOODS TO USE LIBERALLY
FOR DIET LEVELS ONE, TWO & THREE

Fresh fruits and vegetables, especially dark green leaves and deep, yellow fruits and vegetables like pumpkins, papayas, mangoes, carrots, squash, potatoes, etc. Use Whole grain cereals like wheat, buckwheat, millet, barley, cornmeal, oatmeal in their recommended proportions, since they are generally acid-forming. Make free and abundant use of garlic, onions, tomatoes, celery and lemons/limes. These are very therapeutic and health-building. Almonds and Brazilian nuts are the few nuts that leave an alkaline ash in the system and thus are superior to the other nuts. Use them in moderation, however. The nuts should be eaten raw and not roasted. Breakfast or lunch may be heavy, but the evening meal should be light. Fruits, or fruits and cereal are generally ideal.

CONTRAINDICATIONS
FOR DIET LEVELS ONE, TWO & THREE

During Phase One and Two observe the following:
+ Use absolutely no dead flesh. Bury the carcasses in the cemetery and not in your stomach.
+ Use no *dairy or animal products except honey.
+ No cooked foods, except vegetable broths. Drink the mineral-rich broths but do not eat the solids and the small amout (5-10%) of steamed or lightly cooked foods permitted in phase two. Their mineral and vitamin content has already been extracted. They would tax the digestive system almost to no purpose.
+ No butter, margarine, lard or fats, except olive oil and raw nuts (almonds, Brazil nuts)in moderation (5-8). No fried foods.
+ No highly refined, processed fragmented food, especially not white

sugar, white flour, white rice, or their products. Eat natural, whole-grained, high-fiber foods.

♦ No baking powder, soda, MSG., mustard, vinegar (except apple cider vinegar), black or white pepper, or hot spices or rancid foods. Cayenne (capsicum or bird pepper) may be used in moderation. It is medicinal and boosts the circulation.

♦ No excessive use of salt.

♦ No coffee, tea, chocolate, cola or soft drinks. Use fruit, vegetable juices or broths and the herbal teas recommended.

♦ No hurried eating without due mastication. Do not eat and drink at the same time as it dilutes the digestive juices and promotes fermentation and more toxins in the system. Drink 45- 60 minutes before eating, or 1 ½ hours after. If your digestion is normally feeble, wait two hours after. Do not eat between meals. Space your meals at least five (5) hours apart. Eat a few hours before and not just before going to bed.

*NOTE

In poor or developing countries where there is a scarcity of good natural foods and persons are affected by poverty, eggs and milk (especially goat's milk) may be used in Phase Two (2) or Three (3). Great care should be exercised, however, to lessen the danger by securing the eggs or milk from farmers or individuals who are known to raise these animals naturally and in a reasonably healthy and drug-free condition. Two or three eggs weekly would be adequate moderation, since eggs are rich in cholesterol. They should not be fried but boiled or used in the special recipe given for low blood pressure.

* EACH LEVEL of alkaline must be accompanied by maximum output from the organs of elimination. See section on "Enhancing and Maximizing Elimination".

FOOD FOR THOUGHT

"Instead of studying nutrition and diet and detoxification with respect to the human body, we have been studying germs....The world is traveling on the wrong road. Free the body from its toxins and nourish it correctly and the miracle of health will be performed." Dr. Arbuthnot Lan.

Level Two Alkaline Diet

This diet is classified as the CHRONIC ILLNESS DIET and as the terms implies, is indicated for sickness of a chronic nature. It is the second most powerful of the three and offers the same great potential for the fast recovery of health. It is less stringent than Level One, and would therefore, logically take a little longer time to achieve the same results as the first level. Its advantage, however, is that people are more likely to follow it more faithfully, since its time (and obviously discipline) required for using only uncooked foods is for a shorter duration and thus less severely felt. It comprises three phases, like the others, but of shorter duration than Level One.

PHASE ONE
FIRST 15 DAYS DURATION
(From day 1 to day 10 — 15)

+ 100% ALKALINE DIET (can with great benefit also extend for an other 2 —3 weeks).
+ A mono diet (a single kind of food article at a meal) is best. That is, use grapes only ideally (for three meals daily — use the quantity and variety that you desire) for 1-2 weeks. This holds extraordinary cleansing and healing potentials. This is the number one (1) recommendation for those who have the discipline. Grapes, papaya, pineapples, oranges, mangoes, or bananas can also be used with respectively increasing therapeutic and cleansing merit from right to left. In other words, grapes would be the best choice if you can get them, papaya second, etc.
+ Using 100% uncooked foods (fruits or raw vegetable salads), is the alternative to, or second choice in place of the mono diet, follow this for the rest of phase one, after your mono diet terminates.
+ Observe contraindications strictly. See next page. No harmful foods whatsoever!

PHASE TWO
NEXT 30 DAYS DURATION
(From day 16 to day 45)
Steamed or lightly-cooked foods may be used.
The diet should consist of 85% alkaline-forming foods and only 15% acid-forming foods. See the table on alkaline foods on page.
Keep observing your contraindications. Do not fall back.

PHASE THREE
NEXT UMPTEEN DAYS
(From day 46 to indefinite)

+ Use 80% alkaline-forming foods and 20% acid-forming foods. See its table.
+ Eat sensibly and watch those harmful foods. It costs too much to be sick again.

FOODS TO USE LIBERALLY
FOR DIET LEVELS ONE, TWO & THREE

Fresh fruits and vegetables, especially dark green leaves and deep, yellow fruits and vegetables like pumpkins, papayas, mangoes, carrots, squash, potatoes, etc. Use Whole grain cereals like wheat, buckwheat, millet, barley, cornmeal, oatmeal in their recommended proportions, since they are generally acid-forming. Make free and abundant use of garlic, onions, tomatoes, celery and lemons/limes. These are very therapeutic and health-building. Almonds and Brazilian nuts are the few nuts that leave an alkaline ash in the system and thus are superior to the other nuts. Use them in moderation, however. The nuts should be eaten raw and not roasted. Breakfast or lunch may be heavy, but the evening meal should be light. Fruits, or fruits and cereal are generally ideal.

CONTRAINDICATIONS
FOR DIET LEVELS ONE, TWO & THREE

During Phase One and Two observe the following:

* Use absolutely no dead flesh. Bury the carcasses in the cemetery and not in your stomach.
* Use no *dairy or animal products except honey.
* No cooked foods, except vegetable broths. Drink the mineral-rich broths but do not eat the solids. Their mineral and vitamin content has already been extracted. They would tax the digestive system almost to no purpose.
* No butter, margarine, lard or fats, except olive oil and raw nuts (almonds, Brazil nuts)in moderation (5-8). No fried foods.
* No highly refined, processed fragmented food, especially not white sugar, white flour, white rice, or their products. Eat natural, whole-grained, high-fiber foods.
* No baking powder, soda, MSG., mustard, vinegar (except apple cider vinegar), black or white pepper, or hot spices or rancid foods. Cayenne

(capsicum or bird pepper) may be used in moderation. It is medicinal and boosts the circulation.

* No excessive use of salt.
* No coffee, tea, chocolate, cola or soft drinks. Use fruit, vegetable juices or broths and the herbal teas recommended.
* No hurried eating without due mastication. Do not eat and drink at the same time as it dilutes the digestive juices and promotes fermentation and more toxins in the system. Drink 45- 60 minutes before eating, or 1 ½ hours after. If your digestion is normally feeble, wait two hours after. Do not eat between meals. Space your meals at least five (5) hours apart. Eat a few hours before and not just before going to bed.

*NOTE:

In poor or developing countries where there is a scarcity of good natural foods and persons are affected by poverty, eggs and milk (especially goat's milk) may be used in Phase Two (2) or Three (3). Great care should be exercised, however, to lessen the danger by securing the eggs or milk from farmers or individuals who are known to raise these animals naturally and in a reasonably healthy and drug-free condition. Two or three eggs weekly would be adequate moderation, since eggs are rich in cholesterol. They should not be fried but boiled or used in the special recipe given for low blood pressure.

* EACH LEVEL of alkaline must be accompanied by maximum output from the organs of elimination. See section on "Enhancing and Maximizing Elimination".

Level Three Alkaline Diet

This diet is for acute illness and is classified accordingly. It is the least powerful of the three but offers the enough potential for the recovery of health. It represents the minimum level of dietary discipline of the three. It is the least severe of the three, but most likely to be followed by people with very little will power who would perhaps not follow any of the more strict two. If followed consistently, it will definitely restore health, but over a clearly longer period of time. It comprises three phases, like the others, but with the shortest length of time for the first two phases. Its three phases are:

PHASE ONE
FIRST 7 DAYS DURATION
(From day 1 to day 7)

* Use a 100% ALKALINE DIET (can with great benefit also extend for another 1 or 2 weeks).
* A mono diet (a single kind of food article at a meal) is best. That is, use grapes only ideally (for three meals daily — use the quantity and variety that you desire) for 3-7 days. This holds extraordinary cleansing and healing potentials. This is the number one recommendation for those who have the discipline. Grapes, papaya, pineapples, oranges, mangoes, or bananas can also be used with respectively increasing therapeutic and cleansing merit from right to left. Thus, grapes would be the best choice if you can get them, papaya second, etc.
* Using 100% uncooked foods (fruits or raw vegetable salads), is the alternative to, or second choice in place of the mono diet. Follow this for the rest of phase one, after your mono diet terminates.
* Observe contraindications strictly. See next page. No harmful foods whatsoever!

PHASE TWO
NEXT 22 DAYS DURATION
(From day 8 to day 30)

* Steamed or lightly-cooked foods may be used.
* The diet should consist of 85% alkaline-forming foods and only 15% acid-forming foods. See the table on alkaline foods.
* Keep observing your contraindications. Do not fall back.

PHASE THREE
NEXT UMPTEEN DAYS
(From day 31 to indefinite)

* Use 80% alkaline-forming foods and 20% acid-forming foods.
* Eat sensibly and watch those harmful foods. It costs too much to be sick again.

FOODS TO USE LIBERALLY
FOR DIET LEVELS ONE, TWO & THREE

Fresh fruits and vegetables, especially dark green leaves and deep, yellow fruits and vegetables like pumpkins, papayas, mangoes, carrots, squash, potatoes, etc. Use Whole grain cereals like wheat, buckwheat, millet, barley, cornmeal, oatmeal in their recommended proportions, since they are generally acid-forming. Make free and abundant use of garlic, onions, tomatoes, celery and lemons/limes. These are very therapeutic and health-building. Almonds and Brazilian nuts are the few nuts that leave an alkaline ash in the system and thus are superior to the other nuts. Use them in moderation, however. The nuts should be eaten raw and not roasted. Breakfast or lunch may be heavy, but the evening meal should be light. Fruits, or fruits and cereal are generally ideal.

CONTRAINDICATIONS
FOR DIET LEVELS ONE, TWO & THREE

During Phase One and Two observe the following:
* Use absolutely no dead flesh. Bury the carcasses in the cemetery and not in your stomach.
* Use no *dairy or animal products except honey.
* No cooked foods, except vegetable broths. Drink the mineral-rich broths but do not eat the solids. Their mineral and vitamin content has already been extracted. They would tax the digestive system almost to no purpose.
* No butter, margarine, lard or fats, except olive oil and raw nuts (almonds, Brazil nuts)in moderation (5-8). No fried foods.
* No highly refined, processed fragmented food, especially not white sugar, white flour, white rice, or their products. Eat natural, whole-grained, high-fiber foods.
* No baking powder, soda, MSG., mustard, vinegar (except apple cider vinegar), black or white pepper, or hot spices or rancid foods. Cayenne (capsicum or bird pepper) may be used in moderation. It is medicinal and boosts the circulation.
* No excessive use of salt.

- No coffee, tea, chocolate, cola or soft drinks. Use fruit, vegetable juices or broths and the herbal teas recommended
- No hurried eating without due mastication. Do not eat and drink at the same time as it dilutes the digestive juices and promotes fermentation and more toxins in the system. Drink 45- 60 minutes before eating, or 1 ½ hours after. If your digestion is normally feeble, wait two hours after.

Do not eat between meals. Space your meals at least five (5) hours apart. Eat a few hours before and not just before going to bed.

*NOTE:
In poor or developing countries where there is a scarcity of good natural foods and persons are affected by poverty, eggs and milk (especially goat's milk) may be used in Phase Two (2) or Three (3). Great care should be exercised, however, to lessen the danger by securing the eggs or milk from farmers or individuals who are known to raise these animals naturally and in a reasonably healthy and drug-free condition. Two or three eggs weekly would be adequate moderation, since eggs are rich in cholesterol. They should not be fried but boiled or used in the special recipe given for low blood pressure.

* EACH LEVEL of alkaline must be accompanied by maximum output from the organs of elimination.

HERBAL MASTER FORMULAS

FORMULA #1: HERBAL GARLIC SYRUP TONIC

This is one formula that especially emphasizes the great healing virtues of garlic. It combines all the above healing properties of garlic plus those of its other ingredients: Fennel, caraway, apple cider vinegar (very medicinal), honey, and vegetable glycerine. This remarkable combination (along with the fact that the garlic's properties have not been destroyed by heat) makes it a very powerful builder of the immune system. It also helps in all types of respiratory and mucus conditions or ailments. Still further, it helps with weight control, gas and indigestion, female problems, and helps destroy harmful, putrefactive bacteria in the colon, promoting the growth of the beneficial lacto-bacteria. In short, the formula captures all the 'cure-all' virtues of garlic and these powerful synergistic herbs.

Ingredients:
1 pound garlic
3 ounces sweet fennel
3 ounces caraway or anise
3 pounds pure honey
1 quart apple cider vinegar (other vinegars are very damaging to health and red blood cells).

Put the caraway and fennel in the quart of cider vinegar and simmer them for 15 minutes, while covered closely. Now blend the garlic in this liquid and leave the mixture for four days. Shake vigorously each day. After four days add 1 pint of glycerine, and leave for another day. Finally, strain and add three pounds of pure honey. Your powerful master formula is ready for use.

Here is a partial list of the conditions for which garlic is helpful:		
Athletes' foot	Bronchitis	Asthma
Abscess	Chills	Cancer
Boils	Colds	Colic
Colitis	Parasites	Diabetes
Constipation	Earache	Dropsy
Diarrhea	Warts	Emphysema
High blood pressure	Infections	Psoriasis
Low blood pressure	Tumors	Pneumonia
Intestinal problems	Eczema	Infections
Respiratory problems	Fever	Pimples
Sore throat		

WE REMIND YOU THAT GARLIC is one of the most powerful medicinal herbs on planet earth. Did you know that like lemons, it is almost a cure-all? Here is an impressive list of its medicinal properties:

• Anthelmintic, antispasmodic, antibiotic, antiparasitic, carminative, cholagogue, digestive, diuretic, expectorant and febrifuge, resolvent and still others.

Garlic stimulates the activity of the digestive organs, alleviates and corrects poor digestion. It is useful for chronic stomach and intestinal problems, and as an expectorant (expelling phlegm and mucus) it is excellent for catarrh, bronchitis and all problems of the chest and mucus membranes. As a cholagogue, it improves the health of the gall bladder and liver.

Garlic is excellent for all types of infections and especially intestinal ones like: typhoid fever, cholera, dysentery, and dangerous bacteria and parasites. It is excellent for intestinal putrefaction and foul-smelling stool. Garlic is also very effective in lowering high blood pressure and counteracting arteriosclerosis.

DIRECTIONS FOR USING HERBAL GARLIC SYRUP TONIC:
Take one teaspoonful 2—4 times daily with meals. In severe conditions, (colds, coughing, sinus, etc.) you may use it every half hour until relief is obtained. There are no toxic effects even in large quantities.

Supplementary formula to use when items for formula # 1 are not available

FORMULA   #1B: COUGH FORMULA

Ingredients:
1 tbsp. honey
1 tbsp. apple cider vinegar(substitute lemon juice if you can't get cider vinegar)
¼ tsp. cayenne
¼ tsp. ginger
Add two tablespoons of hot water, mix well and take a teaspoonful as often as needed.

MASTER FORMULA #2 THREE-DAY GALLSTONE DISSOLVE

METHOD A:
Day 1: Drink at least 2 quarts of apple juice during the day. Before going to bed mix ½ cup lemon or lime juice with 1 cup olive oil.

Day 2: Take an enema on rising, then repeat the program for day one.
Day 3: Repeat day two's program— The gallstone will by now be dissolved—GONE.

METHOD B:

Drink at least 2 quarts of apple juice for two consecutive days. On the third morning, drink 1 cup lemon juice and one cup olive oil. Now take a garlic enema. Recognize the stones as they pass. They are often black or dark green in color.

METHOD C— (24 HOUR DISSOLVE)

Have a simple breakfast (apples or oranges) and take a colonic or enema after eating. Do not eat again for the rest of the day (you may use apple or orange juice). About 2 hours before retiring, prepare and have ready ½ pint lemon or lime juice and 1 pint olive oil. Now take 2 ounces of the oil and 1 ounce of the juice every 15 minutes until finished. On going to bed, lie on your right side with a pillow under your hips. This will concentrate the mixture and keep it in the gall bladder. When you eliminate next morning the stones should pass

Note:

Substitute pure orange or grape juice if you cannot obtain apple juice, but apple juice is ideal.

MASTER FORMULA #3 (GARLIC COCKTAIL)

Ingredients:
6—10 lemons or limes
1—2 tablespoons honey
Pinch of cayenne
2-3 bulbs of garlic
      Squeeze the lemons into a glass or cup, then peel the garlic and blend them in the lemon juice or chop them very fine. Stir in the honey and let the mixture sit for an hour covered. Then take 1-2 teaspoons alone or in combination as often as needed during the day until finished.

Medicinal virtues

* This is a powerful cleansing tonic cocktail for the body and especially for the respiratory tract.
* It enhances digestion, removes gas and reduces putrefaction.
* It builds up the immune system.

* Supplies important minerals and vitamins for the body.
* Captures all the combined virtues of lemons, garlic, honey and cayenne.

MASTER FORMULA #3B —GARLIC OIL

Here is a simple but masterful herbal formula for making GARLIC OIL.

Peel one pound of fresh garlic and blend it in one quart of pure olive oil. Leave the mixture for 3-5 days in a warm place or sunlight, then strain with a fine cloth or sieve. Now you have powerful garlic oil that combines the benefit of garlic and olive oil.

SPECIFIC USES FOR GARLIC OIL		
Abscess	Asthma	Athletes Foot
Boils	Bronchitis	Cancer
Chills	Colds	Colic
Colitis	Constipation	Diabetes
Diarrhea	Dropsy	Earache
Eczema	Emphysema	Fever
High Blood Pressure	Infections	Intestinal Problems
Low Blood Pressure	Parasites	Pimples
Pneumonia	Psoriasis	Respiratory Problems
Sore Throat	Tumors	Warts
Yeast Infections		

Directions:

For internal use, take one teaspoonful every 2-3 hours or 3-5 times daily. For inflammation of the middle ear or earache, or ear infection: put 4-5 drops of oil into the ear canal and plug it with cotton several times daily. Rub the oil well into the affected area 2-3 times daily for external use ½ oz

MASTER FORMULA #4 —DR. STANFORD'S KURE-ALL BITTERS
(A more potent variation of Swedish bitters)

**FORMULA FOR DR. STANFORD'S
KURE-ALL BITTERS**

VERSION ONE	VERSION TWO
½ oz Hops	½ oz powdered Wormwood
½ oz Wormwood	½ oz Angelica root
1 oz Dandelion root	½ oz Lobelia
½ oz White willow ½ oz Valerian	1 oz Dandelion root
1 oz Red clover	½ oz Myrrh
1 oz Peppermint	½ oz Comfrey root
½ Corn silk; ½ Angelica root	½ oz Rhubarb root
½ Cascara Sagrada	¼ Cayenne ½ oz Parsley
½ oz Mullein ½ oz Marigold	½ oz Senna leaves
½ oz Yarrow; ½ oz Rosemary	¾ oz Ginger
¼ oz Cayenne ¼ oz Cloves or Ginger	½ oz Marigold (Calendula)
½ oz ½ pint Glycerine (optional)	½ oz ½ pint Glycerine (optional)
3 pints grain or sugar cane Alcohol about 40% by volume	2 ½ pints grain or sugar cane Alcohol about 40% by volume

METHOD:
Put all the ingredients in a large glass bottle along with the alcohol and glycerine. Close the bottle and let it stand in a warm place for a minimum of 2 weeks. Shake vigorously each day. Afterwards pour off some for everyday use and leave the mixture intact. The longer this mixture is allowed to remain the more potent it becomes. The portion poured off for everyday use should be put in small dark bottles and kept in a cool place.

USES:
This KURE-ALL Bitters is useful for all pains, and all illnesses internally and externally: for cold, flu, impure blood, lower bowel cleansing, burns, circulation, strokes, kidneys, colic, stomach, neuralgia, heart, the pancreas, skin, joints, arthritis, etc.

Directions:
Use 1 teaspoon 2—4 times daily in hot water or herb tea (Heat evaporates the alcohol very quickly). For external use (on the skin) rub a little oil or cream before applying as alcohol tends to absorb the natural oil from the skin. For use in the ear, put a drop or two of castor oil or olive oil before putting a few drops of KURE-ALL bitters.

WHY IS KURE-ALL BITTERS SO POWERFUL AND VIRTUOUS?
The reason, as you can quickly see, is because the herbs target all the major areas. For example:

* Hops, White Willow and Valerian alleviate PAIN and strengthen the NERVES
* Wormwood, Peppermint, Mandrake, Yarrow, and Dandelion fortify the STOMACH and LIVER.
* Cascara Sagrada, Senna, Mandrake, and Dandelion greatly cleanse the LOWER INTESTINAL TRACT AND COLON.
* Red clover, Marigold, Mullein, Yarrow, and Cayenne help PURIFY THE BLOOD and strengthen the CIRCULATION, the SKIN and other organs.
* Angelica, Rosemary, and Ginger help alleviate FEMALE PROBLEMS.
* Corn Silk and Dandelion are very good for the KIDNEYS AND URINARY TRACK.

KURE-ALL bitters is indeed indicated in all pains and help with all illnesses. Make some at home and you will be glad you did.

THE LEMON-CLEANSE THERAPY

MASTER FORMULA #5

LEMONS/LIMES are among the greatest medicinal fruits in the world, as all experienced natural health authorities will tell you. Used properly, it has been known to effect healing in more than 150 diseases. It has a high vitamin content(B, C) and is rich in the alkaline minerals (calcium, iron and phosphorous). This property makes it an excellent destroyer of toxins, a powerful bactericide and highly effective for acid stomachs. Lemons have innumerable applications that are practical, preventive and very therapeutic.

Note: For people whose system and stomach are very toxic, lemons cannot suddenly be used in large quantities, lest they suffer painful or distressing (though almost never harmful) reactions. For these persons, the stomach-bile barrier can be overcome by the patient and persistent use of lemon juice (diluted in water or tea) in small but gradually increasing amounts.

THE LEMON-CLEANSE THERAPY			
ON DAY	EXAMPLE ONE AMOUNT OF LEMONS	EXAMPLE TWO AMOUNT OF LEMONS	EXAMPLE THREE AMOUNT OF LEMONS
1	2	3	4
2	4	6	8
3	6	9	12
4	8	12	16
5	10	15	20
6	10	15	20
7	8	12	16
8	6	9	12
9	4	6	8
10	2	3	4
TOTAL	60	90	120

THE LEMON CLEANSE THERAPY			
	EXAMPLE ONE	EXAMPLE TWO	EXAMPLE THREE
ON DAY	AMOUNT OF LEMONS	AMOUNT OF LEMONS	AMOUNT OF LEMONS
1	2	2	3
2	3	4	6
3	4	6	9
4	5	8	12
5	6	10	15
6	7	12	18
7	8	14	21
8	9	16	24
9	8	14	21
10	7	12	18
11	6	10	15
12	5	8	12
13	4	6	9
14	3	4	6
15	2	2	3
TOTAL	79	128	192

HOW TO DRINK THE LEMON JUICE

The lemons do not have to be drunk all at once. Each day's supply may be spread out during the 24-hour day, at least during your waking hours. They should be diluted with some water or herb tea, but use no sugar. If any honey is used it should be very sparing. REMEMBER that if your system is very toxic. You cannot start using large quantities, the reactions will be too strong and distressing. Persistently use small but gradually increasing amounts in such a case to build up your tolerance and overcome the stomach-bile barrier.

USES AND CONDITIONS FOR THE
LEMON CLEANSE THERAPY

Acid Stomach	Appendicitis	Arteriosclerosis
Arthritis	Beriberi	Bladder/urinary Problems
Blood-poisoning	Bronchitis	Catarrh
Circulation	Colds	Constipation/colon
Cough	Dandruff & falling Hair	Diabetes
Digestive Disorders	Diphtheria	Epilepsy
Fallen Stomach	Fevers (All Kinds)	Gases
Gout	Gripe	Headaches
Heart/circulation	Hemorrhages	Herpes
Hydropsy	Inflammations	Kidney Diseases/stones
Liver/gall Bladder	Lymphatic System	Malaria
Measles	Nervousness	Obesity
Pleurisy	Poor Appetite	Pox
Rheumatism	Scurvy	Sinus
Snake/insect Bites or Stings	Stomach/intestinal Pains	System Disorders
Tuberculosis	Ulcers	Worms
Wound(all Kinds)		

* For dandruff and falling hair massage the scalp firmly with lemon juice mixed with some onion juice.
* For bites of poisonous insects and snakes, a vast quantity of lemons has been successfully used (30—45 lemons). Bear in mind that the information is offered here for educational purposes. We assume no medical responsibility.

Lemon-cleanse therapy should be accompanied by a diet of mainly raw fruits or vegetables for greatest benefit. By all means ensure that there is maximum elimination, when large amounts of lemons are used. (2 daily enemas, and/or steam baths, etc., during this treatment is recommended, especially when more than seven lemons are consumed per day). If there is not adequate elimination of the toxins and of the morbid wastes pulled out of the system by the lemons, these poisons will remanifest in the form of boils, abscesses, headaches, etc. So ensure that all the organs of elimination are stimulated to work at high efficiency.

HERBAL SKIN SALVE/CREAM

MASTER FORMULA #6

Salve # 1	Ingredients	Substitutes
	Elderberry blossoms	Marigold flowers
	Yarrow	Black walnut or White oak bark
	Red clover blossoms	Plantain
	Golden seal	Wormwood
	Balm of Gilead buds	Comfrey or Marshmallow
	Olive oil / pinch of cayenne	Sunflower or vegetable oil
	Beeswax(optional)	Cocoa fat or butter(optional)
Salve # 2	**Ingredients**	**Substitutes**
	Marigold flowers(calendula)	Yarrow
	Red clover flowers	Dandelion or Burdock root
	Plantain	Black Walnut or Chickweed
	White oak bark	Yellow dock
	Comfrey	Mullein or Bayberry bark
	Olive oil / pinch of cayenne	Sunflower or vegetable oil
	Beeswax(optional)	Cocoa fat or butter (optional)

METHOD:

Simmer about ½ —1 oz of each of the herbs listed or those that you can get (you can make it with only 2 or 3 herbs, if necessary), in 1—1½ pints (²/₃ liter) of olive oil. Use a double boiler (a pot within a pot) to prevent burning. Simmer for about three hours. Cool and strain with a fine cloth. The oil now contains all the medicinal virtues and may be used just like that. To bring it to the consistency of a salve or cream, it is now necessary to reheat the oil and add the beeswax or cocoa butter. Add about 3—5 ozs., depending on the desired consistency. In warm conditions or climate it may be necessary to add a little more. You can experiment with half of the oil first. Only when it is cool can you test the desired consistency.

A tablespoon or two of castor oil may be added to enhance its virtues, also one or two tablespoons of apple cider vinegar. If you desire to have the salve scented, use a few drops of eucalyptus and/or peppermint oil or benzoin or any scented herbal oil or powder that is beneficial and would not affect its healing virtues. Alternatively, a sweet-scented herb like peppermint can be simmered with the other herbs if you do not have scented oils. Mix thoroughly all these ingredients, stirring vigorously if necessary to remove air bubbles or small lumps. Store in a cool dark place. The salve can last for a very long time, without losing much of its virtues.

MASTER FORMULA #7—ANTI-WRINKLE BEAUTY SECRETS
<u>Version A</u>

Ingredients:

½ oz glycerine

½ rose water

½ oz witch hazel

   3 tablespoons honey

<u>Version B</u>

Ingredients:

Tincture of benzoin

½ oz glycerine

3 tablespoons honey

Add a few drops of your favorite cologne if desired.

* Honey and glycerine are excellent and age-old moisturizers.

Other Tips:

* Massage warm olive oil into the forehead. This will help eliminate wrinkles.
* Massage with barley water with a few drops of oil of balm of Gilead (or olive oil as a substitute).
* A fresh papaya is excellent for making your skin soft and velvety. Apply a coat of mashed or blended papaya for 10 minutes. Lie down during this time with your feet a little higher than your head. An enzyme in the papaya will help remove the dead outer layers of skin. After 10 minutes, wash face with warm water then finish with cold water for a few seconds.

MASTER FORMULA #7b —BEAUTIFUL HAIR WASH

* Steep an ounce of rosemary in 1 pint of boiling water. Considered the best hair wash or rinse known, for this reason many commercial hair shampoos contain rosemary.
* Boil a handful of stinging nettles in a quart of water (you may add 2—4ozs of apple cider vinegar) for another excellent hair wash that will also darken grey hair.

MASTER FORMULA #8 —BLACK WALNUT EXTRACT

INGREDIENTS:
>Black walnut hulls (before the nuts ripen)
>Alcohol

Place 3 ozs. of black walnut hulls green, unripe) in 1 pint alcohol (about 40% by volume) and leave for 2 weeks in a warm place, shaking vigorously each day. Then strain and keep in dark brown (actinic) bottles in a cool dark place.

Organic potassium iodide is naturally occurring in the green, unripe husks of this tree. It is a potent remedy for:

Abscesses	Acne	Boils
Diphtheria	Dysentery	Eczema
Itch	Parasites	Prolapsed Uterus
Ringworm	Scrofula	Shingles
Syphilis	Tumors	Worms

Directions
Take 1 teaspoon in a cup of hot water or herb tea 3 times daily. The hot water or tea will cause the alcohol to evaporate. For external use, rub the affected area very well several times daily.

FOOD FOR THOUGHT
Did you know that ALMONDS are king of the nuts? They are nutritious, easily digested and most of all, unlike most nuts they are alkali-forming. Their protein is also superior by far to animal proteins.

TONIC FORMULAS AND HEALTH COCKTAILS

TONIC FORMULA #1—ALKALINE-PROTEIN DRINK

Take 5 —8 almond nuts (or 3—5 Brazilian nuts or an ounce of grated coconut), 2—4 slices of pineapple (or two oranges) and a tablespoon or two of honey, and blend with 1 cup of water in a blender; add a little vanilla or cinnamon. The juice of half a lemon may be added also, if desired. Add one or two tablespoons of dry oatmeal to thicken and enhance mixture if desired.

Pure Nut Milk

To obtain pure nut milk, double the quantity of nuts and honey and leave out the fruits. Add 2 tablespoons of dry oatmeal to enhance and thicken the milk. Remember to put a little bit vanilla or cinnamon. 1-2 tablespoons of flaxseed and/or sesame seeds can also greatly enrich the nutritional value of the milk.

TONIC FORMULA #2—ALKALINE GREEN DRINK

The leaves of many vegetables being very rich in chlorophyll and other nutrients, they are often used to make an excellent "green drink." Using water or unsweetened pineapple juice in the blender select about four to seven of any of the following:

Alfalfa	Barley Grass	Burdock
Cabbage	Carrot/beet Tops	Celery
Chard	Colaloo	Comfrey
Dandelion	Green Onions	Kale
Lettuce	Marshmallow	Nettle
Parsley	Plantain	Pumpkin
Radish Tops	Raspberry Leaves	Spinach
Sprouts	Sweet Green Pepper	Turnip Tops
Wheat Grass		

Directions

Simply blend and strain and drink slowly, try to salivate well. If you have an electric juicer, these greens can be chopped and pressed into the juicer, just like other vegetables. You will then mix about $1/_3$ of green juice with $2/_3$ of beet, celery or carrot juice.

Another method is to first make one glass of juice from carrot, beet and celery and then pour the juice into the electric blender and switch on low. Now feed your available green into the blender slowly. Finally, switch on high and blend very well.

* Again remember that green juice is extremely beneficial in almost all conditions of ill health, as it offers valuable chlorophyll and a liberal quantity of vitamins, minerals, enzymes, trace elements and other healing secrets that as yet only Nature and the Creator seem to know.
* Do not use too many combinations at once if you care about the flavor.
* Be cautious about the leaves of some plants. The leaves of potato and rhubarb, for instance, are poisonous.

TONIC FORMULA #3 — ALOE VERA-CHARCOAL DRINK

INGREDIENTS

> 3-5 teaspoons of aloe vera gel (preferably fresh)
> 2 teaspoons of charcoal (activated charcoal is best)
> 1 teaspoon of molasses
> The juice of half or one lemon added if desired.

Mix or blend together in half a cup of water or herb tea and use once per day. Ideally, take for at least 2 weeks. The tonic may be taken for a month if desired then skip a week or two and repeat. The treatment should be followed by a good purge or colon cleanse.

This treatment is a powerful way to cleanse and strengthen the digestive tract and bloodstream. It also strengthens the immune system and supplies vital nutrients—charcoal is universally known for its ability to absorb and eliminate toxins.

TONIC FORMULA #4 — GRAPE AND EGG TREATMENT

VERSION A

INGREDIENTS

8 ozs. of pure grape juice (can be prepared in a blender/juicer at home or you may use Welch grape juice).

> 1 egg (from healthy uncontaminated, naturally-raised hens).
> A pinch of cayenne
> 1-2 teaspoons of lemon juice
> A dash of garlic powder if desired or a small piece of fresh garlic

Blend together well and drink fresh. Pure orange juice or pineapple may be substituted for grape juice.

This is a very healthy tonic for persons who are very weak or skinny and whose blood-making organs are enfeebled. It is also excellent for low-blood pressure. This treatment should only be for a short period (1 or 2 weeks) since eggs are rich in cholesterol. A week or two may be skipped and the treatment repeated. Some persons half the time use only the egg white in place of the whole egg, if the treatment is for a longer time.

VERSION B
♣Pure goat's milk may be substituted for grape juice in the above formula.

VERSION C
Raw peanut, almonds or Brazilian nuts may be substituted if wholesome eggs cannot be obtained. Do not use a large amount of nuts (1-2 ozs. maximum), and the nuts should not be roasted.

TONIC FORMULA #5 — VEGETABLE BROTH

Chop, cut or grate between 7 and 10 types of vegetables like carrots, sweet potatoes, celery, tomatoes, colaloo, pumpkins (with skins) garlic, onions, beets, cabbage, etc., into small pieces and boil in about 1 quart of water for about 35-40 minutes. This broth is highly ALKALINE and very rich in minerals. When cool strain and use. Do not use the vegetables as they have already lost most of their nutrients to the broth (unless you are making a vegetable soup in which case you should blend them). Drink this broth during the course of the day between meals as often as you like. The body derives great benefit from using this broth which does not have to be digested like the solids. The vitamins and minerals are very easily assimilated and used.

* Use only very little or no salt and no oil in the broth (except a teaspoon or two of olive oil when about to be drunk).
* The broth may be seasoned with your favorite herbs like: Parsley, Oregano, Rosemary, Thyme, Basil, or Cayenne.
* Use no harmful spice like black or white pepper, mustard, MSG, etc.
* The only superior to this broth would be raw vegetable juices made in an electric blender.

TONIC FORMULA #6— NUTRI-SALAD DRESSING

VERSION A
INGREDIENTS
> 1-2 lemons
> 3-4 tablespoons olive oil
> 1 bulb garlic
> — ½ onion
> Dash of cayenne, sea salt or other salt
> 1-2 teaspoons of soy sauce or Bragg's amino acid (optional)

Blend well (add 2 or more teaspoons of water, and/or a little more olive oil if desired) and a piece of celery stalk. Shelled pumpkin seeds are also excellent and nutritious if available.

VERSION B

With the above recipe, include raw cashew, almonds or other nuts and enough olive oil or other good vegetable oil to have the mixture at desired consistency. If no salt is used then honey or dates may be added to sweeten. When nuts are used, a fruit like a banana can be also added to give desired body to the dressing or a tablespoon of dry oatmeal. You can enrich the dressing with a dash of cinnamon, vanilla, ginger or other wholesome seasoning.

* When made thick enough these dressings can be used in place of margarine or butter and is much superior to both.
* These formulas are both very good. The first, is simple and excellent for vegetable salads. Not only does it render the meal more palatable, but it actually facilitates digestion and supplies valuable nutrients. Lemons, garlic and cayenne are good doctors; olive oil lubricates and tones up the digestive tract, as well as help to dissolve gallstones and cholesterol, in addition to being a laxative. The combination is indeed a veritable health dynamo.

FOOD FOR THOUGHT
CHARCOAL is a very effective and harmless remedy for most types of poisoning. Use 2-4 tablespoons depending on the quantity ingested or its severity.

ENHANCING AND MAXIMIZING ELIMINATION

During a cleansing alkaline diet, or "juice fasting," the body undertakes massive housekeeping and cleansing. Consequently, a vast amount of toxins and morbid waste matter are generated. These need to get out of the blood stream and system as fast as possible. Otherwise, they counteract and subvert the healing process and generate great distress. The organs of elimination therefore need every assistance to maximize their efficiency.

These organs are primarily the skin, lungs, kidneys/bladder and the colon.

For the skin Dry Brush Massage (massaging the skin with a dry brush for 10—20 minutes), once or twice a day is very effective. So is also the use of hot and especially cold baths, saunas, hydrotherapy. Whatever promotes perspiration through the skin is very therapeutic and desirable since a large quantity of toxins are eliminated in sweating.

Exercise greatly helps to excrete toxins through both the lungs and perspiration.

Using copious amounts of fruit and vegetable juices or broths, herb teas and pure water, enhances and promotes the work of the kidneys as it eliminates toxins through the urine.

The greatest attention, however, needs to be paid to the colon, since this is where most of the toxins will be found. This is consequently where the vital issue of health and life or disease and death will be determined. In other words, the condition of your colon directly promotes disease and death or health and life.

Since with a proper alkaline diet or juice fasting, massive quantities of impurities are stirred up to be eliminated, mainly through the colon, then not only the anti-constipation regimen must have a high priority, but help here is very essential in the form of colonic irrigations or enemas.

It is highly advisable that during the first week of the alkaline diet (all levels) that enemas should be taken or better twice daily—morning and evening. The more severe the illness, and the stricter the diet—the more cleansing is done and impurities generated. After the first week, the enemas may be reduced or discontinued as the case may be but the bowels must be made to move al least **twice** daily. If a liquid diet (juice fasting) is followed, Then for this **entire** period, 2 enemas daily are recommended.

The herbs that are recommended for the particular condition, are usually beneficial also in the form of enemas. Additionally, some very well-known and very therapeutic enemas include the following:

* Charcoal-2 to 4 tablespoons-to remove toxins; also, excellent for foul odors.

* Garlic —6 bulbs to 2 quarts of water— excellent for infections and parasites.
* Catnip—2 tablespoons, very soothing to the colon and are good for children.
* Slippery elm—2 tablespoons— neutralizes acidity and absorbs foul gas, also excellent for colitis, diarrhea and hemorrhoids.
* Flaxseed tea-¼ cup to 1 quart water-strain and fill bag; very soothing, cleansing and healing.
* Chlorophyll or Swedish or KURE-ALL bitters —2-3 tablespoons— are also often used with very great benefit depending on the problem. They are healing and very cleansing.

FOOD COMBINATION

A GENERAL GUIDE
Did you know that proper food-combination greatly affects health?

Rule 1: Group B mixes with both others. Do not combine items from Groups A and C.

Rule 2: 80% of foods should be selected from the fruits /vegetables' category and the remaining 20% should consist of grains, nuts and seeds from the Group B category which consist of acid-forming foods.

GROUP A	GROUP B		GROUP C
ORDINARY FRUITS	HERBAL FRUITS, SPECIAL FRUITS, GRAINS, NUTS, SEASONINGS, CUCURBITS		ORDINARY VEGETABLES/ GREEN
APPLES	**GRAINS**	**CUCURBITS**	POTATOES
APRICOTS	CORN	CUCUMBERS	ARTICHOKES
BANANAS	RICE	SQUASH	ASPARAGUS
CRANBERRIES	OATS	PUMPKINS	BEETS
DUNKS	WHEAT	CANTALOUPE	BRUSSELS
GENIPS	(CEREALS)	*MELONS	SPROUTS
GRAPEFRUIT			CABBAGE
MANGOES	**NUTS**	**PEAS/BEANS**	CARROTS
ORANGES	ALMONDS	SOY BEANS	CASSAVA/
PEACHES	CASHEWS	RED BEANS	YUCCA
PEARS	BRAZIL NUTS	CHICK PEAS	CAULIFLOWER
PERSIMMONS	PECANS	ALL PEAS/	COLALOO
PLUMS	PEANUTS	BEANS ETC.	DANDELIONS
RAISINS	**HERBAL**	**SPECIAL**	EDDOES
SOURSAP	**FRUITS**	**FRUITS**	KALE
STRAWBERRIES	PINEAPPLE	AVOCADO	LETTUCE
TANGERINES	TOMATOES	PAPAYA	RADISH, ETC.
	EGG PLANT	OLIVES	SPINACH
	PEPPERS, ETC.	COCONUT, ETC.	TURNIPS, ETC.
	SEASONINGS		
	ONIONS/GARLIC/CELERY/ETC.		

*Generally recommended by Natural Health Experts to be eaten alone.

HOW TO COMBINE FRUITS - A GENERAL GUIDE

* "Knowledge in regard to proper food combinations is of great worth, and is to be received as wisdom from God."
* "Read the best authors on these subjects, and obey religiously that which your reason tells you is truth."

Basically, there are 3 main categories of fruit, excluding the nut family fruits. Sweet fruits, Acid fruits and Sub-acid fruits. While many people eat them in any combinations, there are great health benefits to understanding the science of food combinations, even as you avoid both extremes.

For a happy stomach, with more perfect digestion, for a clear brain and efficient memory, observe the following simple rules whenever possible.

ACID FRUITS	SUB-ACID FRUITS	SWEET FRUITS
CITRUS FRUITS	[7]*PINEAPPLES	VERY SWEET
GRAPEFRUITS	*PLUMS	FRUITS
ORANGES	*STRAWBERRIES	BANANAS
PINEAPPLES	APPLES	DATES
PLUMS	CANTALOUPES	FIGS
STRAWBERRIES	GRAPES	RAISINS
TAMARINDS	MANGOES	ETC.
TANGERINES	PAPAYA, PEACH	
ETC.	PEARS, ETC	

♦ Mix sub-acids with any other the other fruits.
♦ Avoid mixing sweet and acid fruits.
♦ While fruits can be used with any grains, acid fruits are best for protein-rich foods.

Be sensible and courteous at all times. Avoid being a "liberal" (anything goes, I don't care), or a "crank" (a fanatic) as Inspiration counsels. Set a right example and don't fight with anyone, just reap the good health benefits and the approval of God and your conscience.

"Read the best authors on these subjects, and obey religiously that which your reason tells you is truth."

---

[7]Some acid fruits, when very sweet may fall in the sub-acid category.

VITAMIN TABLE AND NATURAL SOURCES

Vitamins	Required Daily Amount	Maximum Short term only	DISEASE SYMPTOMS	NATURAL SOURCES
A	800 mcg RE(2700-3300)	25,000—50,000 units	Poor vision, night blindness, low immunity, colds, poor appetite, defective teeth /gums, skin disorders, dry dull hair, dandruff, etc.	Colored fruits and vegetables, esp. Carrots, pumpkins, green leafy vet. (Kale, turnip greens spinach), melon squash, yams, tomatoes, dandelions, etc.
B_1 Thiamine	1.0 mg.	100 mg.	Poor appetite, muscular weakness, slow heart beat, irritability; defective HCL acid, diabetes; mental depression, beriberi, neuritis, edema, etc.	Brewers yeast, wheat germ/bran; rice polishing; most whole-grain cereals, oats and rice; nuts and seeds, beans, soybeans, vegetables Beets, potatoes and leafy vegetables.
B_2 Riboflavin	1.2 mg—1.7 mg	25-50 mg.	Bloodshot eyes; abnormal sensitivity to light, itching, burning eyes; cracks on lips, corners of mouth; dull hair, skin problems, split nails, burning tongue, mouth inflammation, cataract, vaginal itching, etc.	Whole grains, brewers yeast, torula yeast, wh. germ, almonds, sunflower seeds, leafy vegetables, etc.
B_3 Niacin	13—19 mg.	100 mg per meal	Coated tongue, canker sore, irritability, nervousness, skin lesions, diarrhea, forgetfulness, insomnia, headaches, anemia, pellagra, skin problems, depression, dullness, etc.	Brewers yeast, torula yeast, wh. germ, brown rice, peanuts, green vegetables, etc.

VITAMIN TABLE AND NATURAL SOURCES

Vitamins	Required Daily Amount	Maximum Short term only	DISEASE SYMPTOMS	NATURAL SOURCES
B_6 Pyridoxine	1.8-2.2 mg children: 0.3-1.6 mg	200 mg.	Anemia, edema, mental depression, skin disorders, sore mouth /lips, halitosis, nervousness, eczema, kidney stones, colon inflammation, insomnia, tooth decay, irritability, headaches, etc.	Brewers yeast, bananas, avocados, wh. germ/bran, soybeans, walnuts, bl. Molasses, cantaloupe, cabbage, egg yolks, green leafy vegetables, green peppers, carrots and peanuts. Pecans and esp. raw foods.
Folic acid B_9	400 mcg.	5 mg daily	Serious kin disorders, hair loss, poor circulation, fatigue, mental depression, spontaneous abortions, low sex drive in males.	Dark green leafy vegetables (broccoli, asparagus, spinach, etc.) Lima beans, Ir potatoes, lettuce, brewers yeast, wheat germ, nuts, peanuts, etc.
B_{12}	3.0 mcg	50-100 mcg	Poor appetite, sore mouth, loss of mental energy, chronic fatigue, etc.	Sunflower seeds, b. yeast, peanuts, bananas, comfrey leaves, pollen, kelp, raw w. germ
C	60 mg	100-10,000 mg	Soft gums, slow healing wounds, collagen, anemia, infections, scurvy.	Fresh fruits/vegetables, rose hips, citrus fruits, currents, strawberries, broccoli, tomatoes, bell peppers etc.

VITAMIN TABLE AND NATURAL SOURCES

Vitamins	Required Daily Amount	Maximum Short term only	DISEASE SYMPTOMS	NATURAL SOURCES
D	5-10 mcg (200-400 IU)	4000-5000 units	Rickets, tooth decay, pyorrhea, bone, defects, aging, weakness, etc.	Sprouted seeds, fish, liver oils, sunflower seeds, eye bright herb, sunlight.
E	8-10 mg (12-15 IU)	200-2,400 IU	Coronary system problems, strokes and heart disease, abortions, miscarriages, etc.	Unrefined, crude vegetable oils, raw sprouted seeds, nuts, grains, wh. germ oil, g. leafy vegetables and eggs.
K	Unknown		Hemorrhages anywhere in body, nosebleeds, bleeding ulcers, low vitality, premature aging, etc.	Kelp, alfalfa, green plants, soybean oil, egg yolks, by friendly bacteria in colon.

Minerals	RDA	Maximum Short term only	SYMPTOMS	NATURAL SOURCES
Calcium	800-1200 mg women/ kids 1,000—1,400 mg		Osteomalacia and osteoporosis (weak, porous bones), retarded growth, tooth decay, rickets, nervousness, depression, h palpitations, cramps, spasms, insomnia, irritability.	Most raw vegetables, especially dark leafy vegetables Like endive, lettuce, watercress, kale, cabbage, dandelion greens, Brussels sprouts, brocoli, sesame & sunflower seeds, oats, navy beans, almonds, walnuts, millet, tortillas, etc.
Potassium (K)	1,875—5,625 mg		Excess accumulation of sodium (salt) in tissue with poisoning effect, edema, hi blood pressure, heart, failure, low blood sugar, nervous problems, weakness, etc.	All vegetables, esp. green leafy vegetables, oranges, whole grains, sunflower seeds, nuts, potatoes (with skin), bananas, etc.
Phosphorus	800-1,200 mg. Children 1,000-1,400 mg.		Weak bones, retarded growth, rickets, nerve and brain defects, general weakness and reduced sexual power.	Whole grains, nuts and seeds, legumes, egg yolks, dried fruits, corn, etc.
Magnesium	350-400 mg	—700 mg per day.	Loss of body calcium and potassium, kidney damage and stones, muscle cramps, atherosclerosis, heart attack, epileptic seizures, nervous irritability, premature wrinkles.	Nuts, soybeans, raw and cooked leafy vegetables, esp. Kale, endive, chard, celery, beet tops, alfalfa, figs, lemons, apples, peaches, almonds, whole grains, sunflower /sesame seeds, brown rice
Iron	10 mg-males 18 mg-females		Anemia, low resistance, shortness of breath, headaches, pale complexion, low sex drive.	Bananas, peaches, apricots, bl molasses, prunes, raisins, brewers Yeast, sunflower/sesame seeds, rye, dry beans, lentils, kelp, dulse.

Minerals	RDA	Maximum Short term only	SYMPTOMS	NATURAL SOURCES
Zinc	15—30 mg.	600 mg short term	Retarded growth, birth defects, sexual functions, low resistance, white spots on finger nails, toes, etc	Wheat bran, wh. germ, pumpkins seeds, b. yeast sunflower seed, onions, nuts green leafy vegetables.
Iodine	150 mcg. (0.15 mg.)		Goiter, enlarged thyroids, cretinism, anemia, low blood pr. cancer, etc.	Kelp, dulse and other seaweed. Swiss chard, turnip greens, garlic, watercress, pineapples, pears, artichokes, citrus fruits.
Sulfur	unknown		Brittle nails and hair. Skin disorders, eczema, rashes, etc.	Radish, turnip, onions, celery, horseradish, string beans, watercress, kale, soybeans, etc.
Selenium	NA(.05-0.2)		Liver damage, muscle degeneration, premature aging, cancer.	Brewers yeast, sea water, kelp, garlic sea foods, eggs, cereals, most vegetables.

WHAT IS A 'HEALING CRISIS'?

With natural health and nutritional programs, there is usually a notable improvement in health is a short time. However, when a person's body is very toxic, a fasting and/or cleansing program often results in an apparent but temporarily change for the worse, before the marked improvement is noted. What causes this? The reason is simply that the effective cleansing program is dissolving large amounts of accumulated toxins and waste substances and throwing them in the bloodstream in preparation for elimination.

The result is that the eliminative organs the skin, lungs, kidneys, and liver are temporarily overloaded. The large quantities of toxins in the blood stream, cause the disagreeable symptoms headaches, bad breath, skin eruptions, fever catarrh, etc. The good news, however, is that this is something temporary and it can even be slowed down by reducing the intensity of the cleansing for the time.

The healing crisis is a sign of better health, if the program is continued. It shows that the body is really responding. Clients should understand that it is a favorable response from their bodies to the program. Understanding these simple explanations can make an infinite difference in order to keep motivating and inspiring clients.

STAGES IN DISEASE PROGRESSION

Disease naturally goes through stages. It is almost never static over a period of time. When the diseasing-causing factors remain, a disease gets progressively worse. When persons begin cleansing programs, and start changing health-destructive habits, the body begins the healing process. A disease generally begins to reverse the process of its development - to retrace its steps as it were.

Pain actually acts to notify us that there is a problem somewhere in the system usually around the area where it is felt. In this sense, pain is not an enemy, but on the contrary, it acts as a friend to warn us to thus avoid greater injury or even death.

Though we certainly don't welcome pain, it is good to be intelligent as to its function. Without pain we would be unaware that some organs are injured or damaged until it would be too late. People would often drop dead for no apparent reason and with no warning.

Though the pain goes away, a disease as we have seen in the illustration with the cigarette, may be silently and treacherous growing into something worse. Thus the manifestation of pain or disease symptoms need not be looked upon with fatality, but be understood as the body seeking to expel harmful toxins from the system. It is the body's way of saying "help me please, your poor health-habits are overwhelming me with toxemia, lighten my load with good health habits please and help me eliminate the toxins more quickly?"

As a rule this message is generally misunderstood. Persons with the pain and/or disease symptoms rush to the doctor to obtain a drug that will suppress these symptoms. The medication is well calculated to do its job of symptoms suppression and having done so, the patients feel relieved. But are such persons any better with the symptoms now suppressed?

Actually the persons are decidedly worse. Suppression of disease and disease symptoms always produces something worse. It may take even years for the symptoms or suppressed disease to reappear, but repressed disease never fails to remanifest in time as something much worse.

To illustrate, let us take one of the commonest disease manifestations -The common cold. While is really it means that the body is expelling toxins, people generally suppress it with drug medication. So the toxins remain in the system. The drug may seem to work because in time you seem not to get cold, but later yes, you get influenza. With stronger doses or another drug you likewise suffocate it. Now in time come asthma, or lung problems and you repeat the cycle: each time forcing back the excess toxins and frustrating the house-cleaning efforts of the body.

Finally one day, maybe years later, some awful pain drives you to the medical doctor and, you exclaim "Oh, no! This couldn't be happening to me, there must be some terrible mistake, but you know it isn't." The diagnosis? - One of the modern-day killers: heart disease, cancer, diabetes - seems about to shatter your whole life.

This is the horrible cycle of disease manifestation, progression, suppression and fatal remanifestation. Fortunately you can now break this vicious cycle. Invest in health efforts today and reap abundant vigorous health in time.

FOOD FOR THOUGHT

"When I see a uniformed Medical Surgeon on the street, I reflect that this professional knows many ways to amputate my arm, my leg or mutilate my internal organs, but he does not know how to help me keep those organs healthy." Helsby.

REFERENCE LIST

Airola, Paavo. 1990. Are You Confused? Phoenix, AZ: Health Plus Publisher, 1971; reprint.

Airola, Paavo. 1978. How to Get Well. 3 rd ed. Phoenix, AZ: Health Plus Publishers, 1974; reprint.

Azaran, Manuel Lezaeta. 1991. La Medicina Natural al Alcance de todos. (Natural Medicine Within the Reach of All). Mexico, D.F.Impresora Galve.

Bethel, May. 1968. "The Healing Power of Herbs". Northe Hollywood, CA: Melvin Powers Wilshire Book company.

Brandt, Johanna. 1984 (?) The Grape Cure. NY: Ehret Literature Publishing Co., Inc.

Brown, Judith, E. The Science of Human Nutrition. 1990. NY: Harcourt Brace Jovanoich, Inc..

Cantor, Alfred A. Dr. Cantor's Longevity Diet. 1967. NY: Parker Publishing Company, Inc.

Davis, Adelle. 1954. Let's Eat Right to Keep Healthy. NY: Harcourt, Brace and Company.

Houteff, V.T. 1992. The Entering Wedge-The Genesis of Diet and Health. NY: Universal Publishing Association, 1946; reprint.

Jarvis, D.C. 1958. Folk Medicine. NY: Henry Holt and Company, 1958; reprint.

Jensen, Bernard. 1988. Foods that Heal. NY: Avery Publishing Company.

Kellogg, John Harvey. 1903. Rational Hydrotherapy. Philadelphia: F.A. Davis company.

Kloss, Jethro. 1988. Back to Eden. New revised edition. CA: Back to Eden Publishing Company, 1946; reprint.

Lust, John. 1979. The Herb Book. NY: Bantam Book, Inc, 1974; reprint.

Malstrom, Stan. 1977. "Natural Herbal Formulas". Orem, Utah: Fresh Mountain Air Publishing Company.

Meyer, Joseph E. 1986. The Herbalist. Revised enlarged edition by Clarence Meyer. IL: Meyerbooks, 1934; reprint.

Royal, Penny C. 1976. "Herbally Yours". Hurricane, Utah: Sound Nutrition, 1994; reprint.

Ruben, David. 1977. The Save Your life Diet. NY: Ballantine Books, 1975; Reprint.

Sehnert, Keith. 1975. How to be Your Own Doctor. NY: Grosset & Dunlop.

ABOUT THE AUTHOR

Dr. Errol Stanford holds a Ph.D. degree in Nutrition Counseling in addition to being a Naturopathic Doctor. (N.D.) Educated in the United States and South America and having traveled extensively for many as a Health practitioner and lecturer, all across the continental United States, Europe, Mexico and South America, Dr. Stanford brings considerable wealth of knowledge and experience to bear in this book. He is currently the director of the Sunny Mtn. School of Natural Medicine, Mountaindale, New York 12673 —A school for promoting Natural Health internationally, through external studies or correspondence programs.

That you may find these short, but profound, gems of sufficient practical interest and good common sense to motivate you to a healthier lifestyle, is Dr. Stanford's sincere desire and prayer.